Pictorial History of the Schwaben Creek Valley

Steve and Joan Troutman

an imprint of Sunbury Press, Inc.
Mechanicsburg, PA USA

an imprint of Sunbury Press, Inc.
Mechanicsburg, PA USA

FIRST DISTELFINK PRESS EDITION: March 2026

Set in Adobe Garamond | Interior design by Crystal Devine | Cover design by Lawrence Knorr | Edited by Lawrence Knorr.

Publisher's Cataloging-in-Publication Data
Names: Troutman, Steve, author | Troutman, Joan, author.
Title: Pictorial history of the Schwaben Creek Valley / Steve and Joan Troutman.
Description: First trade paperback edition. | Mechanicsburg, PA : Distelfink Press, 2026.
Summary: Steve Troutman details the history of the villages along the Schwaben Creek in the greater Mahantongo Valley of Pennsylvania, famous for its Pennsylvania Dutch culture and painted furniture.
Identifiers: ISBN : 1-979-8-88819-262-7 (softcover).
Subjects: HISTORY / United States / State & Local / Middle Atlantic.

Designed in the USA
0 1 1 2 3 5 8 13 21 34 55

For the Love of Books!

Table of Contents

Foreword

The Schwaben Creek Valley parallels the Line Mountain which forms the northern boundary of the Mahantongo Valley in Northumberland County, Pennsylvania. The valley remains agricultural with several villages located along the stream.

The ten-mile-long valley was settled soon after it was purchased from the Indians in 1749 by the Penn Family.[1] The area was attractive to the pioneer families and remains scenic today with a combination of forest and field.

The Pennsylvania German culture is predominant today, as it was in the past. The Pennsylvania "Dutch" language was most used by the early people of the valley. Many school age children learned to speak the English language when they attended school.

Hopefully, the readers of this book, both local and country-wide, will gain an appreciation for the heritage. You will follow the Schwaben Creek from its origin in Leck Kill, in the eastern Mahantongo Valley to its western end at Red Cross. At this western point is where the Schwaben Creek ends and its waters join the Mahanoy Creek and the waters then flow into the Susquehanna River.

1. Treaty with the Indians of the Seneca Nation, held at Philadelphia, July 1, 1749.

The Land of the Schwaben People

An explanation of the origin of the name associated with the title of this book is in order. Many folks realize that the Schwaben Creek took its name from Swabia, an area in Germany. Indeed, there are many immigrants in our Schwaben Creek Valley who may be identified as Swabians. However, it may be a surprise to know that Swabia is not a political area. It has no exact boundary lines or governing body. Swabia is a geographical area.

> Bianca Klinger, of Germany, has visited the Mahantongo Valley many times. She remarks that many Swabians settled in the Mahantongo Valley and built some of the traditional, wonderfully ornamented and painted wooden furniture. You very likely know that the *Swabelaendle* (the area where the Swabians lived) never was an owned state. Their area is limited from the Black Forest in the West, Lake Constance and the Alps in the South, the rivers Lech and Woernitz in the East, and finally

the Hohenlohe-Franconian Plain and the Heuchelberg area in Baden in the North. Thus, the bigger part of Swabia is situated in Baden-Wuerttemberg and a smaller part in Bavaria. The Swabians share a strong cultural identity and their dialect, even though there are many varieties.

Leah M. Specht[2]
November 15, 2025

1917 calendar photo, F. L. Kehres and Son, General Merchandise and Country Produce, Rebuck, PA. Shipping Point, Dornsife, PA.

2. Fourteen years old.

Introduction[3]

In the 18th Century, America's largest colonial minority formed as thousands of Germans and German speaking Swiss found their way into southeastern Pennsylvania. Although these people came from every German language area of Europe and included descendants of French and other peoples who had settled in Germany after The Thirty Years' War (and who had adopted the local cultural and speech), so many came from the Rhenish Palatinate that the term *Pfalzer,* or in English, *Palatine* came to be used to describe them all.

Faced with so large a movement of peoples from one area to another, the English settlers in Pennsylvania had a variety of reactions. The government required them to swear allegiance to the British crown and forswear other loyalties-no problem to most of these folks who were apolitical in their orientation. One of the country's leaders, Benjamin Franklin, frustrated by the Germans' tenacious hold on the language and lifestyle they brought with them, brusquely dismissed them as "Palatine boors."

Benjamin Rush wrote a sympathetic essay about the Pennsylvania Germans and struggled valiantly to establish an institution of higher learning to escort them into the mainstream of the Anglo-American culture. Dickinson College and Franklin and Marshall Colleges resulted from these efforts.

For all the British problems with the Pennsylvania Germans, even they would have agreed with the sentiment placed in the Lutheran liturgy in 1788; "Since it has pleased thee, especially through the Germans, to turn this province into a blooming garden . . ." For German thrift, industry, and ambition were major factors in the economic success of Pennsylvania. And that fact, more than any other, betrays the reason for the migration of these folks. To be sure, the Palatinate and other areas of emigration have been victimized by war and plague and changes in political jurisdiction. But people managed to live through it all, and gradually in the last decades of the 17th and first decade of the 18th centuries, they were rebuilding their shattered world.

Had it not been in the nature of the human soul to long for a better world, a warmer, brighter place in the sun, these Germans might have stayed in their continental villages, subsisting as best they could. When William Penn extended an invitation to his property in America—in person during visits

3. Edited for this publication.

to the Rhineland—when books and letters found their way, even to the valleys of the western Palatinate, a catalyst was provided. By fair means and foul, peasants found their way to Pennsylvania. They were not wrong in dreaming; many of the first generation acquired land in quantities they never could have obtained in Europe. And the land was only one factor in prosperity that provided a new comfort to their lives.

Comfort, however, does not fully extinguish the dream of an even better life; in fact, it may feed it. As a result, the Germans who peopled Pennsylvania's interior also moved on and on. As Indian threats diminished, valleys beyond the gentle Blue Mountains, opened to settlement, and eventually, borders to the west of Pennsylvania were crossed as burgeoning population and good-life-hungry souls moved on.

Pastor Frederick S. Weiser
Lutheran Minister

Kehres Store and Hotel, Rebuck, Pennsylvania. The store front sign says, "Union House."

Geography and Immigration

The Schwaben Creek Valley lies within the northern portion of the larger Mahantongo Valley in Northumberland County, Pennsylvania. The Schwaben Creek flows westward into the Mahanoy Creek at Red Cross, formerly Mahanoy. The mingled waters enter the Susquehanna River at Herndon. The long ridges that define the Mahantongo Valley and the Schwaben Creek Valley are physical boundaries. The ridges dividing the valleys have created settlement areas with unique cultural characteristics within the larger Mahantongo Valley.

The earliest settlers of Central Pennsylvania followed an Indian trail from the home of Conrad Weiser in the Tulpehocken Valley to Shamokin (now Sunbury), the seat of local Indian government.[4] The Tulpehocken Path, as it was known, crossed through the mountain pass in Mahantongo Mountain along the Pine Creek, at a gap, at which the villages of Erdman and Klingerstown stand as sentinels on north and south, respectively. The Pine Creek confluence with the Mahantongo Creek, is at Klingerstown. The Mahantongo then flows west to the Susquehanna River and drains the eastern and southern portions of the valley.

The Tulpehocken Path led travelers north from Klingerstown into the Hoofland Valley. One branch of the Tulpehocken Path divided at the Hoofland Valley and crossed the Hoofland Mountain into the Schwaben Creek Valley.[5] The crossroads community of Greenbrier is now established at this junction of the Tulpehocken Path and the Schwaben Creek. Some settlers also entered the eastern end of Mahantongo Valley by crossing over the Mahantongo Mountain. These folks established their homes in the upper portion of the Mahantongo Valley, locally known as "the Kettle," drained by the Mahantongo Creek. The Little and Big Mahantongo Creeks flow west to Klingerstown.

4. The Six Nations of Iroquois, also known as the Haudenosaunee Confederacy, governed from Onondaga (Syracuse, New York) via their regent, Shikellamy.

5. See the book *Tulpehocken Trail Traces* by Steve Troutman.

LECK KILL

Origin of the names Leck Kill and Schuylkill

"Old Timers will tell you that Leck Kill got its name from the salt licks that once attracted herds of deer that were killed by the early settlers of the area."[6] The deer were attracted to the salt licks and they were killed. They came to *sleck*[7] and were killed as they *slecked* the salt. The German word for lick is *lecken.*

For further consideration: The word "Kil" means "stream." This word originates with the Dutch settlers from the Netherlands. They settled near the Delaware River in the early 1600s. Therefore, using this terminology Leck Kill could be translated "Licking Stream."

Another example from the Dutch settlers of the Netherlands, is the word Schuylkill, which means "Hidden Stream." The Schuylkill River and its tributaries flow south across the terrain now known as Schuylkill County. A southern portion of the Mahantongo Valley lies within Schuylkill County. The Schuylkill River flows south to Reading and Philadelphia, where it joins the Delaware River. Throughout much of its northerly sources, it is bounded by forests and the arching trees which restrict the view of this hidden stream.

Leck Kill Tavern, Store, and Post Office

The hotel in Leck Kill was established in 1825 by Peter Beissel (1801-1873).[8] It has been a licensed place ever since. The building, 76 x 45 feet in diameter, and western part which is of stone has stood for fully one hundred years. The eastern part was constructed some years later. The post office was established by Emmanuel Giest. The place is the business center of the township and for many years has been the polling place.

In the fall of 1900, Daniel S. Leitzel purchased the old established store and hotel stand in what is known as Leck Kill, having the only licensed place in the township of Upper Mahanoy. Daniel S. Leitzel married Annie M. Geise, of Gratz, December 25, 1883. Mr. Leitzel has been the hotel keeper, store keeper, and post master since the spring of 1901. Patronized by the traveling public and residents of the locality, all have a good word for Mr. and Mrs. Leitzel. The

6. Andrew Heintzelman, *The Citizen Standard*, July 31, 1992.

7. Pennsylvania Dutch for lick. Pennsylvania Dutch is a term that refers to the language of descendants of German-speaking immigrants who settled in Pennsylvania between 1683 and 1820.

8. Floyd's *Genealogical and Biographical Annals of Northumberland County*, 1911, pgs. 917–918.

This photograph is of great interest to people associated with the Village of Leck Kill. The scene as found on the internet is from a post card but without any data or information. The picture was taken by a professional photographer for an unknown occasion.

building is now heated with steam. Daniel S. Leitzel was instrumental in the establishment of the Mahanoy and Mahantongo Telephone Company, held the office of treasurer of the township, and is a member of the Masonic Lodge at Shamokin, and Eureka Lodge #260 IOOF of Leck Kill. The Leitzels are members of the Lutheran congregation of St. John's Church, Upper Mahanoy Township.

The ancestry of Daniel S. Leitzel includes the pioneer family who settled on the Mahantongo Creek west of Hebe in Northumberland County. Gottfried Leitzel (1770-1848) married Magdalena Wagner (1769-1840). They are buried in Hebe. Benjamin Leitzel (1803-1881), son of Gottfried, married Elizabeth Byerly (1808-1891). George B. (1830-1881), son of Benjamin, married Christina Schmeltzer (1833-1863). Daniel S. Leitzel, son of George B. Leitzel, was born November 18, 1859, in Jordan Township, on the pioneer homestead of Gottfried Leitzel.

Prior to his ownership of the Leck Kill business place, he had conducted the business at Farmer's Hotel in Shenandoah and the Marshall House in St. Clair. It the fall of 1900, he purchased the old established store and hotel in Leck Kill.

The post card scene[9] includes five people, all male. Two of the men, and a young boy, are dressed in white shirts, with trousers including a belt at the waist. These could be Leitzel family members. Perhaps Daniel S. Leitzel, hotel proprietor, stands in the center of the photo with Ray G. Leitzel, his son,

9. Photo circa 1901 when Daniel S. Leitzel became the store, hotel, and post office operator. Photo analysis by the author.

holding the team of horses hitched to a covered wagon. Emmanuel Leitzel, born 1869, is a younger brother of Daniel S. Leitzel. He is recorded as marrying Rosa Moyer and moving to Leck Kill in 1909. He may be standing to the right, leaning on a hitching post. There are two men dressed in bib overalls. These may be Geist family members. A recent Geist family member, Paul Geist, was the owner, operator of this Leck Kill business. He was a stout man, similar to the older man in bib overalls, standing next to Daniel S. Leitzel. Perhaps Emmanuel Geist and Daniel S. Leitzel pose as close associates. Both men stand at the center of the photo with their hands on their hips. The men on the right side of the photo stand more informally, leaning on a hitching post and a porch railing.

The old stone tavern in Leck Kill was built by Peter Beissel in 1825 as a hotel. It was operated by the Geist family as a bar room, post office, and general store. Paul Geist was the last owner operator. Mary Geist, and daughter in law, Shirley Geist and Paul were the last postal officials. The building is presently a residence consisting of four apartments under new ownership.

Photo, taken in 1992, features, left to right, Shirley Geist, who began serving as postmaster in 1973, Mary Geist, who served as postmaster from 1947 to 1973, and Paul Geist, owner-operator of Geist's Store and Tavern, where the post office was located.

Hoch's Garage, Leck Kill, Pennsylvania

Mr. Schenckweiler built a mill on Schwaben Creek where the Village of Leck Kill became established. It stood east of the old stone tavern and post office. Mr. Hoch's automobile repair shop and garage now occupy the place where the mill stood. The mill was water powered with three sets of stones. A mill dam ponded the water from a tributary of the Schwaben Creek flowing between the tavern and the garage. David Hoch states that the mill dam was located where the garage is now. In 1890 William Kehres operated this mill.[10]

Hoch's Garage.

10. Bell's *History and Biography of Northumberland County, Pennsylvania*, p. 710.

Woodrow and Pearl Kauffman's Store and Ice Cream Parlor

Woodrow and Pearl Kauffman of Leck Kill had a store and ice cream parlor. Many people stopped here to have ice cream and soda. The Clement Masser family stopped on the way home from attending church at St. John's Reformed Church in Leck Kill. This was prior to the building of the new Christ Church in 1952. Woodrow served the refreshments. Benches were available to sit on. Often the girls and ladies would leave the ice cream shop to visit Pearl in the adjoining kitchen. Gas pumps were out front. A few grocery items were sold including soap.

Mark Masser recalls the purchase of bar soap at Halloween time. Mark had attended an evening mid-week viewing for old Eddie Snyder with his parents Pauline and Clement Masser. After the viewing, Mark was obligated to go to catechetical led by Reverend Yarborough. Having no time to change, Mark went to class in his Sunday suit. Betty (Masser) Martz also attended class. Mark and Betty were cousins. Betty and others had planned to soap the Leck Kill school house windows after their catechetical class. Mark had to be careful not to get his suit dirty. The Leck Kill Elementary school windows were duly soaped as a Halloween prank. A group of older and younger kids participated in the event. The next day, Betty was cornered in school and approached as one of the tricksters. She admitted to helping. The Halloweeners

were told that they had to wash the school house windows. After school, Betty came over the hill from the Clarence Masser farm with her daddy's market truck. The huckster truck was loaded with apples and most likely cider. All the kids had a good time washing the windows with plenty of treats, courtesy of Betty's father.

Bryant Klinger and Earl Zartman were frequent customers at Kauffman's. Bryant recalls visiting often during the weekend for ice cream and soda and sitting on the bench.

Wilmer Brown had a woodworking and repair shop east of Kauffman's. When something needed repaired, which was beyond

This building was first the Pine Park High School, second, the Leck Kill Elementary School, and most recently it was converted into a retirement facility owned by Dr. Jamie Reed (2025).

her ability, Mrs. Pauline Masser would say, "I guess we need to take it to Wilmer Brown." Wilmer was the uncle of Luther Brown who lived on the farm east of the Christ Church.

The Christ Church building was established on the drainage divide between the Mahantongo Creek and the Schwaben Creek. Rainwater that falls on the eastern church roof flows into the Mahantongo Creek. Rainwater that falls on the western church roof flows into the Schwaben Creek.

Christ Evangelical and Reformed Church, Leck Kill, Pennsylvania

Christ Evangelical and Reformed Church was dedicated on October 18, 1953. The congregation came into being on February 19, 1950, as a merger of Jacob's congregation at Line Mountain and St. John's congregation at Leck Kill. The members of both congregations voted unanimously in favor of the merger. Jacob's Church, always better known as its local name, Howerter's, had its beginning as a Union Reformed and Lutheran Church in the year 1803. The original log church was erected in 1807. In 1893, the old church was replaced by a more modern structure, which had a separate large room for the use of the Sunday School. This building was used by the Union Church until it was destroyed by a fire on September 23, 1943. The Jacob's Reformed Congregation then accepted the invitation of the St. John's people to worship with them in the building at Leck Kill. The two Reformed Congregations worshipped together until the merger in 1950 made them one. St. John's Church, formerly known as the Little Brick Church, was organized in 1853 by Reformed and Lutheran members who separated from the Himmel's Church at Rebuck. The original church building, in continuous use until 1953, was completed in December of 1853. It was razed in 1958. Soon after Jacob's and St. John's congregations merged in 1950, they began planning to relocate and selected the present site, one mile east of Leck Kill. Mr. and Mrs. Wilson Brown donated land for the new church half way between the meeting place of the time, and the site of the old St. Jacob's Church. It is interesting to note that this hilltop location was chosen to join two congregations from the same locality, but from different watersheds. Rain water which falls on the east church roof finds its way to the Mahantongo Creek. St. Jacob's was in the Mahantongo Valley. Rain water which falls on the west church roof finds its way to the Schwaben Creek. St. John's was in the Schwaben Valley.

Deihl's School

This one-room school was located on lands earlier owned by the Deihl family. Presently the building is located on Upper Mahanoy Township Road east of the Upper Mahanoy Township maintenance shed. Steve Mattern is the owner and has kept the building in good conditions. The building is presently used for equipment storage.

An early reference to the Deihl family can be found in *Genealogical and Biographical Annals of Northumberland County.*[11] Valentine Paul, the pioneer who settled in Northumberland County, Upper Mahanoy Township, located at the source of the Greenbrier Creek, owned a large track of land some of which he cleared and put under cultivation. In 1805 he purchased 120 acres in Mahanoy Township (now Upper Mahanoy) for 550 pounds lawful money from Phillip and Magdalina Deihl. The same year Philip and Magdalina Deihl and their son Micheal Deihl and his wife Magdalina sold a second track, lying against to the one just mentioned, to Valentine Paul. Among the descendants of this family is a daughter Catherine who married John Deihl. These tracks of land are in the vicinity of Pine Park Apartments, which was earlier the Pine Park High School and recently the Leck Kill Elementary School.

11. By Floyd, 1911, pg. 831.

Line Mountain Werewolf: Truth or Legend[12]

LECK KILL—Taking aim by the light of the moon, one night long ago, a Northumberland County farmer fired his rifle at a wolf. Trailing blood, the animal ran off. The next day, the farmer tracked the blood and found the body not of a wolf, but of a man many people had suspected of being a werewolf.

This supposedly happened in lower Northumberland County—in the valley drained by the Schwaben Creek, east of Herndon and south of the Line Mountain. Here's the story, written by Henry W. Shoemaker and excerpted from a 1951 edition of a publication titled *New York Folklore Quarterly*: "May Paul was a 12 year old shepherdess on the Schwaben . . . tall, slim as an aspen twig, with laughing hazel eyes, small lips always smiling, her dark brown curls hidden under her wooly shepherd's cap . . ." To guard her sheep she only had a shepherd's wand and a small dog.

An old man . . . "Suspected by many of being a werewolf" . . . was in love with her, much to her parents' displeasure. He would sit with her on a log at the sheep walk for hours without saying a word. But because no wolves troubled May's flocks, her parents tolerated him.

Wolves from Line Mountain would raid all the other farmers' flocks, "even in

12. John L. Moore, *The Daily Item*, Sunbury, Pennsylvania, October 30, 1986.

broad daylight." Then one moonlit night, "someone shot a gaunt old wolf crossing the road . . . It hobbled down into the Schwaben woods. Next day, the man went to find the wolf for the $25 reward, tracking it by the blood. Instead, he found the Paul girl's aged lover stretched out, lying on his back, shot through the heart."

"It was noticed that his teeth were long and yellow like a wolf's, and that there were stiff hairs on the underside of his hands and on his ears, and on the soles of his feet . . . They buried him where he was found, and the spot is called Old Wolf's Grave "or (in Pennsylvania Dutch) *die woolfman's grob*."

After this, May Paul remained in the Schwaben Valley but details of her life are sketchy. "All that is known is that she never lost a sheep or lamb from the wolves, which for the next quarter century were a terror to the farmers in the Schwaben Valley."

Additional information as told by Parsett Snyder: The werewolf was buried further down the valley, north of the Himmel's Church. The burial location, on a hillside, was marked for many years by a wooden marker which stood in a meadow north of the Schwaben Creek covered bridge.

"In the time frame of 1800 to 1880, every farm kept at least a small herd of sheep for their own wool production," says William Wiest of Dalmatia, an attorney with a keen interest in local history. Old court records and tax records that deal with farms in lower Northumberland County often refer to sheep and wool he says.

Wolves once roamed throughout Central Pennsylvania. Up until the 1870s wolves were considered to be a problem to anyone trying to develop a homestead and raise domestic stock. To eradicate them, many county governments offered cash bounties.

Bill, subsequently employing his legal skills in the courthouse at Sunbury, has delved into the old property records in the Schwaben Valley, looking for material that would discount or substantiate the story. One finding: Back in the 1800s, a farm just east of Leck Kill, now owned by Mark Gessner, was once owned by a man named Michael Paul. Records in the Orphans Court listed a Tobias Paul among Michael Paul's children. In turn, the county registrar's docket carried the names of Tobias's children. Among them was a daughter, Lillie May Paul.

Upper Mahanoy Township, Northumberland County, Office and Equipment Shed[13]

Officers in 2025: Supervisor Brett Kahler, Chairman; Supervisor Gary Kahler, Vice Chairman; Supervisor Eric Klinger, Road Master; Eric Kahler, Secretary/ Treasurer.

13. 126 Upper Mahanoy Township Road.

Leck Kill International Order of Odd Fellows Lodge Hall[14]

Vickie and Brad Wiest live next door to the east of the IOOF Lodge Hall, in Leck Kill, Pennsylvania. Vickie has been a resident of this community all her life. She recalls a globe sign above the door entrance way. It was inscribed with the letters IOOF. In more recent times this was the polling place where elections were held. Community members came here to vote. Jeff and Traci Farrell now own this property. They live next door to the west. Rodney and Leah Unger previously owned the lodge hall and the Farrell residence.

Conversation with Darlene (Giest) Masser, age 79, of Leck Kill provided the following information. Darlene is a lifelong residence of the neighborhood. She recalls the lodge had many social events which promoted community service. Annual suppers were held including an oyster and a turkey supper. The meals were prepared on the first floor where the tables were arranged. Square dances were popular in the lodge hall. While the adults danced downstairs, a play area for the children was provided upstairs in the lodge meeting area. The young folks danced upstairs while the older folks square danced downstairs in the social hall. The square dancers travelled to other locations to provide entertainment.

The lodge had its own musicians. Some of the names of the musical group were, Lawrence Snyder, Marlin and Harry Kieffer, Walter Wiest, and "Lut" Williard. The lodge square dance group wore special attire, full skirts and "cancan" petticoats were the women's attire. Some of the dancers included Guy and Mae Schreffler, Lester and Alma Geist, Bud and Lila Geist, Delphine and Harvey Brown. Some of the additional lodge members recalled are, Irvin Schreffler, Woodrow Mattern, Alan Dieter, Joe Hornberger, Earl Oxenrider, Cletus and Ruth Fetter, Pat and Marion Latsha, Darwin Schreffler.

Geist General Store Warehouse and the Old Reitz Residence

This warehouse was formerly an Eastern States Feed distribution center. The feed distributed from this building, originated at other milling facilities.

Geist Store Merchandise warehouse and the old Reitz homestead occupy the center of Leck Kill.

14. Eureka Lodge #260, active into the 1950s.

Geist General Store was directly across the street from the warehouse. The store was also the location of the Leck Kill Post Office and barroom. This was operated for many years by the Geist family. The store, bar room and post office fronted the highway side. The store and post office entry door was separate from the barroom entrance.

The Reitz homestead is the present-day Conrad residence. It was for many years the home of David and Jane Blair.

Former Reformed Church Parsonage, adjacent to Pine Park Apartments, 2010

Wilmer Brown's Blacksmith and Repair Shop

St. John's Lutheran Church, Leck Kill, Pennsylvania

St. John's Lutheran Church, Leck Hill, Pennsylvania, Fall 2024

Former Lutheran Church Parsonage, Leck Hill, Pennsylvania, Fall 2024, located east of the church.

History of St. John's Church, Leck Hill, Pennsylvania

St. John's United German Reformed and Evangelical Lutheran Church was established in Upper Mahanoy Township, Northumberland County, Pennsylvania. This was a union church.

This church known as the Little Brick Church was organized in 1853, by Reformed and Lutheran members who separated from the Himmel's Lutheran and Reformed Church near Rebuck, Pennsylvania. The original building was completed in December 1853 and was in continuous use until 1953. The building was razed in 1958. The Evangelical Reformed Congregation of St. John's, merged then with the Reformed congregation of St. Jacob's (Howerter's) Church near Pitman, following a devastating fire on September 3, 1943. A new church was built to accommodate the merger. Christ Evangelical and Reformed Church was dedicated October 18, 1953. The St. John's Little Brick Church bell, now hangs in the Christ Church belfry.

The St. John's Lutheran Congregation found their new home east of the Little Brick Church. Two cemeteries are established next to each other. The corner stone of the present St. John's Lutheran Church in Leck Kill is carved, "Erected 1914-Rebuilt 1941."

It was appropriate that this church was built of brick, as there are several homes along the Schwaben Creek Valley Road that are composed of brick. This was the building material of choice in this era.

St. John's Church of Leck Kill, the interior of the Little Brick Church.

St. John's Union Church, the Little Brick Church, steeple replaced the first time, 1913-1915. The steeple was replaced the second time in 1928-1929, giving the church a gothic appearance.

Bill Beissel-Faith Healer

William Beissel was an especially noteworthy citizen of Leck Kill. William and Annette Beissel are buried at St. John's Cemetery. Their monument in the old St. John's Cemetery records William Wilson Beissel (1867-1957) and Annette (Wehry) Beissel (1868-1959). William and Annette lived on the Chestnut Ridge, which separates the Mahantongo Creek watershed from the Schwaben Creek watershed. William is descendant from Jacob Beisel, an early pioneer and Revolutionary soldier, with a rank of lieutenant. The Jacob Beisel house is gone, but a large, beautiful stone chimney marks its former location along Knorr Hollow Road. The Jacob Beisel home and log barn was a showpiece in its day. The barn includes a stone forebay with wooden doors and ornate iron hardware. The hardware was forged by a blacksmith. Jacob Beisel (1758-1829) married Gertrude Wagner (1760-1859). Jacob and Gertrude are buried at St. Jacob's (Howerter's) Cemetery, Line Mountain, (between Leck Kill and Pitman).[15]

William and Annette lived one quarter mile north of the Jacob Beisel homestead. William's residence was on Old State Road, which follows the crest of Chestnut Ridge. This dwelling still stands in disrepair. Some outbuildings referred to as house barns, remain also. These were buildings used by the faith healer. Bill was widely known as a faith healer. Some folks refer to this as the art of Pow-Wow. Many local people patronized him and folks travelled from out of the area for his services. Bill was the first official Pow-Wow doctor in the Leck Kill area. He recorded his recipes for physical, mental, and spiritual disorders, in a book he wrote himself entitled, *Secrets of Sympathy*. William Wilson Beissel's book has been reprinted entitled, *Pow-Wow Power: A True Story of a Pow-Wow Relative and Other Related Events*, by James D. Beissel.[16] A quote from the foreword states: "The patient can be successfully helped if he or she has faith in the Trinity and believes these sympathies."

Faith healing involves the knowledge of recipes to cure various ailments. Passages from the Bible are often a part of the cure. Passages are read by the caregiver in a unique fashion providing sympathy. In order for the cure to be effective, the patient needs to be baptized and professed to be a Christian. Some of the people known by your author who were helped by Bill Beissel's faith healing were Joyce Kahler and Ada Troutman. This tradition is locally well known as a source of medical help, not unique to the Beissels. Sally (Wiest) Troutman of Klingerstown and Salome (Bohner) Masser of Leck Kill also performed faith healing practices, mostly within their own and neighboring families.

William and Annette Beissel's home and Bill's house barns located on Old State Road, south of Leck Kill, west of the intersection with Salem Road, July 2010.

15. *The Johannes Jacob Beisel Family History*, by Florence Young, Ruth Kauffman, and Paul E. Troutman, Jr., provides family history. For more information contact Paul E. Troutman, Jr., 3242 Blue Rock Rd., Lancaster, Pennsylvania.

16. It was published in 1998 by Crystal Educational Counselors, Willow Street, Pennsylvania.

Zion School, Upper Mahanoy Township

This residence, once a one-room school house, is located at the intersection of Schwaben Creek Road and Run-A-Buck Road, between Leck Kill and Greenbrier.

The old school house is situated within a cluster of dwellings.

Kaufman (Kufman) Grist Mill

Tom Klinger, of Colorado, is a native son of the Schwaben Creek Valley. His father, Albert Klinger, was a one-room school teacher. Albert taught school at Diehl's and Paul's in the late 1930s and the early 1940s. The Albert Klinger family lived on a farm lately recalled as where Forrest and Reah Miller lived. Brandon Miller and family, a grandson, is the current resident. Tom Klinger recalled his Schwaben Creek homestead to be the location of a grist mill. According to the 1858 and 1875 residence maps for Northumberland County, this grist mill belonged to J. H. Kaufman. There is evidence of a mill dam across a tributary to the Schwaben Creek. This northerly flowing tributary in a long hollow, was impounded by an earthen dam breast still visible on the south side of Schwaben Creek Road. The area behind the dam breast is now a flat field, where ponded water once stood. Conversation with Brandon Miller, confirmed the location of the grist mill as being situated between his home and the Schwaben Creek in the lowland, near the creek. A mill race carried the water from the mill dam across Schwaben Creek Road, through Brandon Miller's yard, down to the mill. The water turned a water wheel, which provided power to turn the mill stone. Brandon Miller has a mill stone in his yard.

Kaufman's Mill Dam Breast south of Schwaben Creek Road at Brandon Miller's. The earthen mound impounded the water where the flat field is seen center photo.

Two grist mill stones are set on top of one another to grind flour. The top stone which rotated is called the runner stone. The lower stone, which did not turn, is called the bed stone. Water exited the mill via a short race which led to the Schwaben Creek. Tom Klinger recalls this mill race behind their home when he lived there. He also recalls the presence of clay along the stream and finding broken tobacco pipes and stone points made by the Indians.

Bell's 1891 *History of Northumberland County*, identifies Charles Kauffmann as a resident of Mahanoy Township in 1778. Daniel Kauffmann of Upper Mahanoy Township was born in 1804, son of Leonard Kauffmann and Mary (Ressler) Kauffmann. John R. Kauffmann, son of Daniel, was born in 1828 in Upper Mahanoy Township and became a prominent business man in Lower Augusta Township.

Brandon Miller and Albert Klinger recall the legend that this place was the site of an early Indian trading post during the French and the Indian War. Local militia may have attended gatherings here as a troop mustering place during the Revolutionary War era. A French coin dated 1738 and an iron cannon ball, two inches in diameter, attest to the above legend. Other artifacts include metal tableware and Stone Age arrowheads made by the Native American Indians. An 1858 map of Upper Mahanoy Township shows a grist mill (G.M.) and sawmill (S.M.) at this location, with the name J. H. Kufman.

A short distance to the east, where Leck Kill is established, another gristmill is identified with the name Shankweiler. Shankweiler's mill was also located on a northerly flowing stream which was a tributary to the Schwaben Creek. The 1858 Map of Washington Township identifies the location of a clover mill near the center of Greenbrier, a blacksmith shop, and a school. A clover mill used mill stones to clean the seeds and separate the seeds from the chaff. The 1875 map of Mahanoy Township shows the gristmill of J. H. Kaufmann. The 1875 map showing Leck Kill includes the Lutheran and German Reformed Church, a hotel and post office and Eureka Lodge #260, chartered on the 16th of August 1847.[17] The mill at the

The grist mill was located photo center, where Brandon Miller has constructed a fire ring. The mill was powered by running water which flowed through a race across the lawn to this location.

The Kaufman's Mill stone displays a small canon ball on top. The mill was in the lowland field in the distance. The canon ball was found in the area of the mill.

Leck Kill Post Office was operated by William Kehres in 1891. A stone tavern at Leck Kill Post Office was built in 1825 by Peter Beisel and was occupied as a hotel. The 1875 Map identifies an oil mill in the center of Greenbrier. An oil mill produced linseed oil by crushing flax seeds with a grist mill stone that rolled on its edge in a stone trough.

Paul's School

Paul's School is also known as Paul's Academy. It was located on Old State Road in Upper Mahanoy Township, Northumberland County. The school was established on land provided by David Paul. The school house was removed by Willard Kahler. He built a new house where the school stood. Willard was the son of Norman Kahler and Mildred (Mattern) Kahler. Norman Kahler purchased the farm from the descendants of David Paul. The Kahler farm, house and barn were located east of the school. John Wehry, Jr., is the present owner of this farm.

Paul's School about 1916.

This photo is courtesy of Gayle Rebuck who has family members who attended this one-room school. Gayle (Paul) Rebuck identifies Charles R. Zartman, Gayle's grandfather, as the student in the front row, second from the left. She estimates the time of the photograph to be prior to 1916. Charles R. Zartman lived with his parents, Joseph R. Zartman and Lizzie (Heim) Zartman. Their Zartman home was located on Salem Church Road, lately recalled as the Amelia Erdman farm. This farm is north of Salem Church. Gayle recalls the last teacher of this one-room school was Roy Bingaman in 1945.

According to Bell: "The public school system was adopted on the 4th of June 1866. The first board of directors was composed of Daniel F. Geist, President, Daniel H. Geist, Treas., David W. Paul, Sec., William Smith, Isaac Kieffer, and Jacob Klock. The number of school buildings is 6 of which 3 were purchased from subscription school trustees, one was built in 1867 and two in 1868."[18]

The secretary named above, David W. Paul, was the landowner in Upper Mahanoy Township who provided the location for the establishment of the public school on his land. The school became known as Paul's Academy. The building previously existed as a subscription school with the Evangelical and Reformed Church, as identified on a map dated 1858.

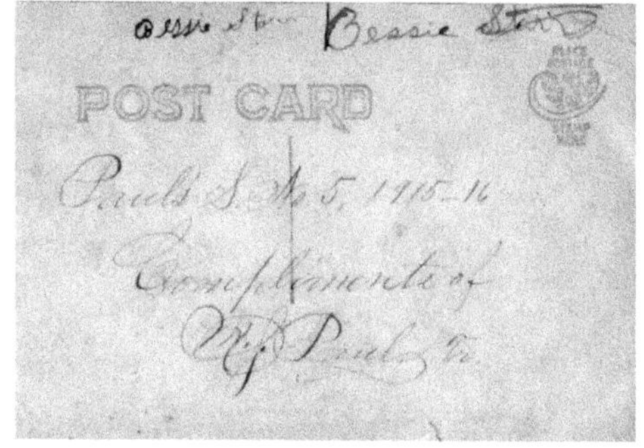

This post card picture of "Paul's Academy" is courtesy of Mary Straub, of Hoffman

18. Ibid.

Road, Upper Mahantongo Twp., Schuylkill County, Pennsylvania. The name Bessie Starr is written on the back of the postcard. Bessie Starr is the daughter of John and Harriet Rebuck Starr and the sister of Mary Jane Starr Hoffman. Mary Jane is the wife of Harvey Clair Hoffinan who was a well-known mechanic and blacksmith back in the day in the Klingerstown area. Mary Straub, granddaughter of Mary Jane and Harvey Clair Hoffman, provided the Paul School postal card information in September of 2024. The reverse of the card states as addressed by the teacher, "Paul's S. #5, 1915-16. Compliments of M.S. Paul, Tr."

The photo postcard was given to Bessie by her teacher, Milton S. Paul. He lived locally on what is now named Corner's Road. Milton lived on an old Knorr homestead where Beatrice Paul was the last to occupy the dwelling. The house still stands in a pasture on the Ken Smith farm. This farm is on the north side of the hill adjoining Benigna's Winery.

The scene is of a group photo including the teacher and twenty-four students. It must have been a cold day when the photographer visited the school Every boy and girl is wearing a substantial coat and the girls all have head coverings of hats and scarfs. Some boys are holding hats as well as the teacher is holding his hat by his side. The schoolhouse looks like a typical German wooden sided one roomer, with wooden shutters. This is a rare photograph. It is the only known photo of Paul's one-room school, locally known as "Paul's Academy."

Pauls' Academy was located on Old State Road. Khristyn Maurer's residence is presently located on this site.[19] Willard and Joyce (Jones) Kahler built this house using some of the recycled wood from the old school Willard dismantled the school when he built a home for himself. Willard attended this school as a young boy. Willard grew up on the nearby Norman Kahler farm. Norman and Mildred Kahler had a large family. The Norman Kahler farm was earlier owned by David Paul, and then by his son, Charles Paul. Norman and Mildred Kahler purchased the farm from Charles Paul during the depression years. The plot of land for the schoolhouse was provided by David Paul

Willard recalled his teacher, John Clark, was a strong man. He often walked to school barefoot, even in the wintertime. John lived several miles away from the school on the farm lately occupied by Lee Clark, between Greenbrier and Leck Kill. Willard said he once climbed a tree at the school house to get away from Mr. Clark, the teacher, who wanted to discipline his student.

Conversation with Gayle (Paul) Rebuck has provided the identification of student Charles R. Zartman. He is the first in the back row, next to the teacher. Charles R. Zartman

19. 1994 Old State Road, Dornsife, Pennsylvania.

is the son of Joseph R. Zartman and Lizzie (Heim) Zartman. This family lived on Salem Church Road at the residence lately recalled as Amelia Erdman. In 1945, it is noted that Roy Bingaman was the teacher at this school.

Line Mountain Post Office

An undated photograph of the Line Mountain Post Office, Northumberland County, which operated at this building until 1932 when it was permanently closed. This post office was located about midway between Pitman, Schuylkill County, Pennsylvania, and Leck Kill, Northumberland County, Pennsylvania. The people on the porch are unidentified but could be the family and employees of G. W. Paul, postmaster, who operated a general store and barroom here.

Geist School

The Geist School is now part of the property of Paul Reiner. It has succumbed to the test of time, and a recent storm has done this deed. The once one-room schoolhouse building is located on State Route 3010 just west of the previous Geist Store of Leck Kill, Upper Mahanoy Township, Northumberland County.[20]

The Geist School house and the Geist School group photo courtesy of Gayle (Paul) Rebuck. The students are identified as follows: Front Row: Luke Kauffman, Daniel Kritzer, Paul Erdman, Marvin Keim, Howard Kritzer, Paul Keim, Ray Erdman. Second Row: David Blank, Dale Kahler, Ruth Schoffstall, Verna Clark?, Esther Rebuck, Margaret Reitz, Leah Reitz, Betty Lou Marie Heim, Ruthann Falck. Third Row: Martha Tobias, Helen Geist, Myrtle Brosius, Edith Erdman, Leroy Heim, Glen Falck, Ken Kahler. Fourth Row: Willard Kahler, John Reitz, Charles Falck, Charles Heim, Earl Reitz, Harry Heim, Teacher, Mary Ziegler

20. Photos courtesy of Gayle Rebuck.

GREENBRIER

Edward Snyder of Greenbrier recalled the oldest grist mill in Greenbrier was across the creek from the newer Brosius cement block mill built in the center of the center of the village. The older water powered grist mill stood on the north side of Schwaben Creek, a short distance downstream from the newer mill. Eddie Snyder recalled the old mill was converted from water power to a gasoline engine power unit. The mill workmen were putting gasoline in the power unit when spilled gasoline caught fire and the old mill burned down. Eddie says he was about two years old when this happened. The year of the fire is estimated to be 1936. The old mill stood near the township road, named Mill Road. It connected the mill in Greenbrier to a mill across the Line Mountain on Mahanoy Creek. Therefore, the road was named Mill Road.

The Village of Greenbrier takes its name from Greenbrier Creek, a tributary of the Schwaben Creek. Greenbrier Creek flows in a northerly direction through the center of the village.

Brosius Mills, Greenbrier, Pennsylvania

The old and the newer grist mills in Greenbrier were built and operated by the Brosius Family. Henry (Hen) Brosius built the newer cement block mill. Hen Brosius also owned an International Harvester dealership across the road from the mill. Trucks and tractors were sold. Henry sold the mill to Ray Klock, close friend and husband of his daughter, Jean.

Daniel (Danny) Snyder Sr. was the most recent mill operator. Chicken feed was a good seller.

Mr. Teter, the present owner of the property, tore the mill down in December 2019. Mr. Teter sold the equipment out of the mill to people from "down south."

Eddie Snyder, who lived next to the mill, said the building materials were salvaged by Amish workers. They took the wooden timbers and steel to Mt. Pleasant Mills, Pennsylvania. When the work day was over, they took truck loads home with them.

Customers recalled the beautiful wooden floor boards inside the mill.

The Geist Relations-200 Years in America by A. Frank Geist was published in 1940. Many Geists have their family tree roots in the Schwaben Creek Valley between Leck Kill and Greenbrier. According to *Geist Relations*, "Father Andrew Geist settled at Greenbrier where he owned close to 300 acres of land and raised a family of seventeen children. An account is given concerning the origin of the name Greenbrier. This section of the country, along the Schwaben Creek, was full of nothing but green briers therefore it was called Greenbrier. These green briers were cleared away and the settlers soon had nice farms along a creek known to them as Schwaben Creek, named after the Swabian Germanic tribe."[21]

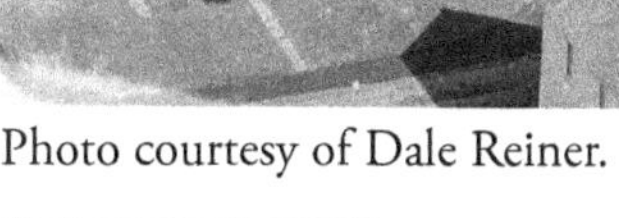

Photo courtesy of Dale Reiner.

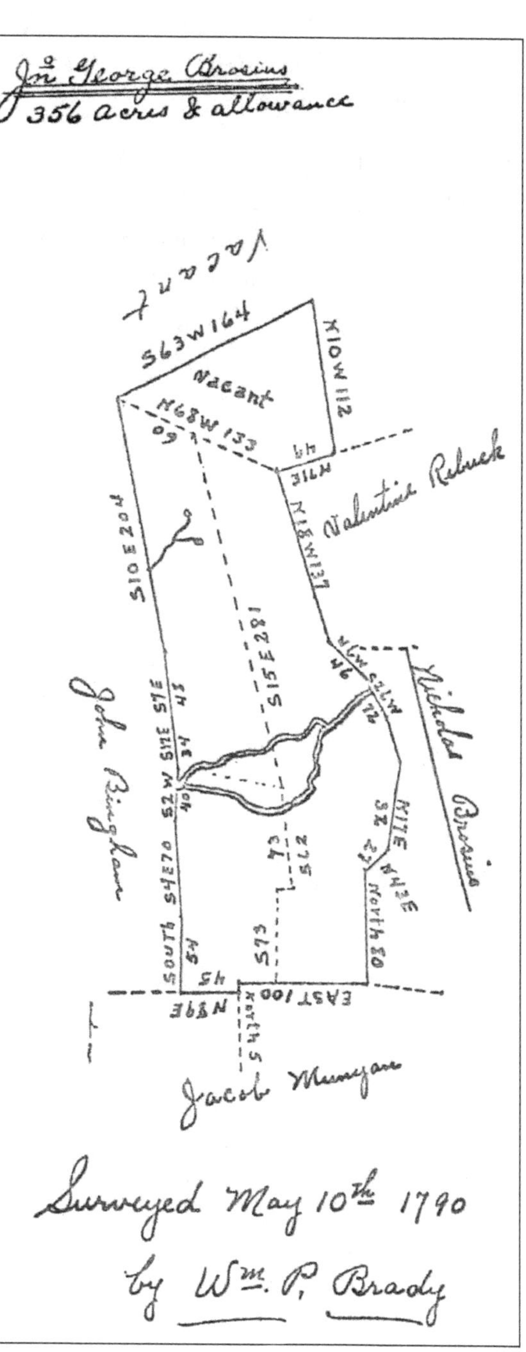

John George Brosius warranted land where the Village of Greenbrier is today. This survey was completed in 1790. Neighboring land owners are identified, including Valentine Rebuck (Hunter's Junction Road), Nicholas Brosius, Jacob Munyan and John Bingham, along the Schwaben Creek.

21. Pg. 217.

Greenbrier School, October 10, 1947

Brier School Road leads to the one-room school location. The road is located near the center of Greenbrier, where the old mill stood. This road leads to the school which was on the north side of Schwaben Creek. Evelyn (Adams) Harner attended Brier School as part of her childhood education. The water bucket was carried on a stick by two people to the school house. It was carried from the Snyder farm next to the mill, back to the school.

First Row: Clarence Snyder, Norman Rothermel, Ed Schlegel, Robert Brosious, James Brosious, Paul Snyder, Forrest Snyder, James Adams.

Second Row: Eleanor Adams, Ruth Snyder, Jeanette Kauffman, Martha Brosious, Jean Rothermel, Romaine Kauffman, Virginia Brosious, William Phillips.

Third Row: Jeff Snyder, Norman Adams, Lena Snyder, Evelyn Adams, Leah Snyder, Mark Brosious, Teacher, Robert Kauffman.

Photo courtesy of Dale Reiner. Identification of names by Evelyn (Adams) Harner and Ruth (Snyder) Macoviak.

Greenbrier Lodge Hall[22]

Greg Erdman lives at the intersection of Greenbrier Road and Schwaben Creek Road in the center of Greenbrier. He lives in the home of his grandparents, previously the Paul Rebuck residence. The Greenbrier Lodge Hall is also known as Greenbrier Grange Hall. The hall can be seen from Greg's residence. This community building was still in use in the 1990s as the home of the Greenbrier Community Band. Some of the band members were Paul Billow, David Snyder, Jim Snyder, and Danny Snyder and others. Danny operated the feed mill across the street, originally named Brosius Mill.

The Boy Scouts also utilized this building. Rebuck Troup 311 met in the grange hall for many years. A new Boy Scout meeting place has been constructed in the grove at Himmel's Church. Henry Brosius's garage can be seen in this photo. The old Henry "Hen" Brosius garage and grange/lodge hall are owned by Adam Wolfgang.

The old Brosius Garage and the Greenbrier Grange/ Lodge Hall.

22. Interview with Greg Erdman, age 69, and Fred Kehler, age 76, autumn 2024.

Photo courtesy of Dale Reiner. Newspaper source.

Greenbrier Store and Post Office. Note the Bell Telephone sign. The store keeper and his wife greet their customers from the porch steps. Photo courtesy of Dale Reiner.

Adams Family History

The Adams Family history is compiled in the book *Genealogical and Biographical Annals of Northumberland County.*[23] This comprehensive history includes several Adams families who emigrated to the Schwaben Creek Valley. The following edited material pertains to one branch of this large family. The Bernhard Adams branch of this family lived between the villages of Greenbrier and Rebuck. This branch includes three successive generations of the name Bernhard.

The county history records . . . Adams or Adam, there are numerous representatives of the Adam or Adams family in Northumberland County. Its history in America goes back to the first half of the 18th century, when Anthony Adam, a potter by trade, emigrated to these shores. He sailed from Rotterdam on *Molly*, commanded by Captain John Cranch, which vessel arrived at Philadelphia, and the passengers, having taken the oath of allegiance to the English Sovereign, were qualified to land October 26, 1741. Anthony Adams' age is entered on the passenger list as twenty-five years, and one account says he was born in the Fatherland (Germany), another that he was a French Huguenot. On February 7, 1748, he received a warrant for a tract of 136 acres of land in Albany Township, then a part of Philadelphia County. This land was surveyed for him June 6, 1752. He was a settler there in 1752, and

On August 5, 2018, a lovely, but hot Sunday afternoon, Evelyn (Adams) Harner traveled with Steve, Val, Emma and Leah to visit Evelyn's childhood homes. These homes were located near the Village of Greenbrier, Pennsylvania. Greenbrier is on the Schwaben Creek, between Leck Kill and Rebuck. Evelyn's parents, Howard "Hop" Adams married Emma (Kahler) Adams and lived on a farm located on what is now named Rothermel Road. Nevin Rothermel purchased the Adams homestead farm from Clemens Adams. Marlin (Mutt) Rothermel is the current farm owner.

23. By Floyd, 1911, pgs. 847–850 and 634–636.

he witnessed and participated in the trying times of the French and Indian Wars.

The date of death of Anthony (or Andoni, as he wrote his name) Adam, of Albany Township, is not known. Neither do we know the name of his wife. But it is known that he had sons: Abraham, Anthony, Bernhard, and Peter.

Bernhard Adam, son of Andoni, was a pioneer in Northumberland County, settling in Washington Township, on the farm now owned by a descendant, Adam Cornelius Adams, and tenanted by the latter's son, Clements I. Adams. It has been in the family for five generations. Bernhard Adam followed farming. He and his wife clung to the Reformed faith and are buried at Himmel's Church.

Bernhard Adam, son of Bernhard, was born May 14, 1793, in Berks County, Pennsylvania, and coming to what is now Washington Township, Northumberland County, married Salome Ferster (or Furster), who was born June 3, 1796, and died Nov. 19, 1846. He died August 25, 1864, and they are buried at Himmel's Church, where they worshipped, being members of the Reformed congregation. Bernhard Adams served that church officially many years, as deacon, elder, and trustee. He was a farmer by occupation, owning the homestead of his father, a tract of 139 acres, now owned by Adam Cornelius Adams. On that property he built a barn which was destroyed by lightning in the nineties. He took great delight in hunting and shot a deer in the district where many of his descendants now live. A bear was also one of his hunting trophies, and he bore an excellent reputation as a marksman.

Bernhard Adam, son of Bernhard and Salome Adam, was the third of the name to own the homestead farm. He was born November 5, 1827, in Washington (then Jackson) Township, and died on his home farm in that township, October 17, 1905. A lifelong farmer, he prospered in his work to the extent that he acquired three farms. He was an active member of the Reformed congregation at Himmel's Church, attending services regularly and holding all the church offices. His wife, Matilda (Zerfing), daughter of Jacob Zerfing, whose wife was a Klock, was born March 25, 1832, and died September 3, 1899. They were the parents of sixteen children.

Adam Cornelius Adams, son of Bernhard and Matilda, also was a substantial farmer of Washington Township, was born August 10, 1863, on the old homestead of the Adams family. He obtained his education in the township schools, was reared to farm life, and assisted his father in horse dealing, butchering, and huckstering in his earlier manhood. In the spring of 1888, he began farming for himself, at the place where he now lives, a farm of 108 acres which formerly belonged to the Reitzes, first to Phillip Reitz, and later to his son, Andrew Reitz. It is on the road between Rebuck and Greenbrier. Mr. Adams remodeled the house and enlarged it, and in 1908, he built an addition to the large barn, erected by Phillip Reitz, who also built the house. Mr. Adams also owns his father's old homestead of about 138 acres, which adjoins his own home farm, and which is one of the most valuable tracts in the township. His son, Clements, now cultivates it. Mr. Adams has held the position of supervisor of the township. He and his family are Reformed members of Himmel's Church, which he served as deacon and elder for a number of years.

On July 1, 1887, Mr. Adams married Mary Crissinger, daughter of William and Susanna (Rebuck) Crissinger of Washington Township, and they had four children: Clements I., George C., Eugene F., and Mamie S. Clements I. Adams, who farms the old Adams homestead, married Annie Adams of Shamokin, a very distant relative.[24]

The Adams family history compiled in *Genealogical and Biographical Annals of Northumberland County* describes another family branch. Nicholas Adam, the ancestor of a large number of this name, was a native of Berks County born July 5, 1758, and coming to Northumberland, settled in the Swabian Creek district, in what is now known as Washington Township. He was a farmer and one of the most extensive land owners in this section. He died April 11, 1826, and is buried at Himmel's Church or in a private burial ground.

Gideon Adams, son of Nicholas, was born in the Swabian Creek district, was a plasterer and followed his trade in addition to farming, having a tract of 120 acres located along the Middle Creek in Washington Township.

Jeremiah Adams, son of Gideon, is buried at Himmel's Church, of which he was a Reformed member. He was the owner of the homestead farm, now the property of Helena Troutman.

Clemens and Anna lived in the big farm house lately known as the Nevin Rothermel residence, 2009.

Howard Adams, son of Clemens, and his wife, Emma Kahler, lived in the small house on the south side of Rothermel's Road lately known as the Marlin (Mutt) Rothermel house. This is the house where Evelyn (Adams) Harner was born.

Evelyn Mae Adams, March 4, 1953.

24. As named above Dr. Eugene Adams (Dentist) suggested the earlier pronunciation of the surname Adams was pronounced "Adum", similar sounding to the season of the autumn.

Clemens and Anna built this retirement home on their 300 acre farm.

Presently this is known as the Leah Shade residence located ½ mile west of Greenbrier on the road to Rebuck.

Adams family residences on both sides of the Greenbrier-Rebuck Road, presently Leah and Richard Shade live on the north side, and the Matthew Snyder family on the south side.

Howard and Emma Adams lived for some years in the farm house across the road from Clemens and Anna Adams. The Howard Adams family later moved south to the old Adams homestead where Evelyn was born.

Clemens I. Adams (January 1, 1888-November 28, 1979), age 91 years; Anna (Adams) Adams (January 10, 1890-April 4, 1960), age 70 years.

Ten children: Francis, adopted girl; Sydney Mary, md. Oscar Brown; Russel md. Ruth Wertz; Howard (Hop) md. Emma Kahler; Irvin md. Pauline Snyder; Josephine md. Guy Erdman; Eugene md. Lena Crissinger; Annable md. Roy Feese; Marvin md. Miriam Shadel; Barney md. Lena Strohecker

Mount Mahanoy and Mahanoy Creek water gap at Dornsife is seen from the former Daniel Kahler farm location.

Kahler Homestead: West past Rebuck turn on Cherrytown Road, turn on first road on right. Farm on left side of road. Earl Kieffer farm now Mark and Paul Kieffer farm. Kahler Family Tree: 1st Andrew Kahler, 2nd Daniel Kahler, 3rd Emma Kahler Adams, 4th Evelyn Adams Harner, 5th Julie Harner Specht, 6th Timothy Specht, 7th Emma Specht

Left to right: George Kahler (son); Harry Rebuck (Son-in-law); Andrew Kahler (Father) 1847-1917, 70 Yrs.; Harvey Kahler (George's son); William Kahler (George's son); Mable Kahler (Harry's wife); Edna Kahler (Daughter-in-law); Mary Kahler (Mother) 1851-1926), 75 Yrs.; Jane Kahler (George's wife).

Daniel Kahler farm on Shaffer Road TR 358, south of Rebuck Pa. Emma (Kahler) Adams, daughter of Daniel Kahler and Rosie Hoffman.

Daniel Kahler and Rosie (Hoffman) Kahler. They had four sons, and five daughters: Harry, Howard (both died young), Robert, Jennie, Nora, and Mary, Claude, Helen, and Emma. Rosie (Hoffman) Kahler (March 30, 1879 – June 10, 1954). Parents were Jacob Hoffman and Sarah Gonser. Daniel Kahler, (1875-1947) was the son of Andrew Kahler (1847-1917) 70 years old, and Mary Kahler (1851-1926), 75 years old. Daniel and Rosie are buried at Himmel's Church. Their daughter, Emma, md. Howard Adams.

Daniel Kahler farm now Rodney Snyder in 2009.

Farm house now Rodney Snyder residence.

Some of the children of Daniel and Rosie Kahler. Mary, Nora, Jennie, Claude, and Emma.

Elderly Emma (Kahler) Adams, daughter of Daniel and Rosie Kahler.

The Adam's Family Farm of past generations. It is presently owned by Marlin and Joan Rothermel. Note the barns are different. The earlier barn burned down. The new barn is the largest in Washington Township

REBUCK

Origins of the Village of Rebuck

The Village of Rebuck in Northumberland County is located in the Schwaben Creek Valley. Rebuck takes its name from the early pioneer Valentine Rehbock, who emigrated to Pennsylvania from Bieber, Germany. Bieber is located in the Spessart region east of Frankfurt. The book *Pennsylvania German Pioneers* by Strassburger and Hinke, has recorded that in 1765 the ship *Chance* landed in Philadelphia. Among the 78 men who are recorded as passengers, is the name Valentine Roeback. In 1774, Valentine Rehbock, is listed as married taxable resident of Augusta Township, Northumberland County. The Schwaben Creek Valley was within Augusta Township at that time.

Rebuck reunions were held at Himmel's Church beginning in 1929. In 1983, Bonnie Lee Raybuck Jones attended these Rebuck reunions. She presented information connecting Valentine Rehbock with a village named Bieber in Deutschland. Bonnie also said Valentine was a miner by trade. Earl G. Troutman and Marion (Romberger) Troutman attended these Rebuck reunions with Earl's mother, Mary (Rabuck) Troutman. With this new information about Valentine's occupation and ancestry, Earl was determined to locate the Village of Bieber in Germany. Earl and Marion had a friend, Philip Klinger of Weinheim, Germany. He was a well-known Klinger historian. Phillip agreed to search for Bieber, the Rebuck ancestral home. Phillip found three villages named Bieber. On the November 9, 1984, Phillip had a reply from a researcher, Ernst-Ludwig Hoffman of Biebergemund, Germany. He had located the correct village in the province of Hesse-Hanau, with the knowledge that Valentine was a miner. Philip replied to Earl on December 11, 1984, that he had found Valentine Rebuck in the Bieber Reformed Kirchenbuch. This church book was dated 1724-1785. The Village of Bieber, in the Spessart region of Germany, east of Frankfurt, was a mining community where gold and silver and other metallic ores were mined underground.

In 1995, Earl Troutman and family of Rabuck descendants visited this ancestral home site. Bieber is a small village nestled in a land that is very hilly with small mountains. The mayor of the village offered a tour. There are restored mines able to be viewed as historical sites and the mayor pointed out a house, still referred to as a Rehbock house. There are very small deer in the locale. These animals have horns and are referred to as a *Rehbock*. Rehbock is defined by Langenscheidt's *German-English Dictionary* as a fawn-colored doe deer, thus the origin of the names Rabuck, Rebuck, Raybuck, Rehbock.

Bonnie Lee Raybuck Jones compiled *Early Rebuck Genealogical History and Maiden Name Lines* in 1985.[25] Your author's line of descendants include: Andreas Rehbock, md. Catherine Elizabeth, d. 1758; Valentine Rehbock, md. Anna Barb. Balduf; Johann Adam Rehbock, 1763-1835, md. Maria Haubt, 1763-1830; Godfried (Little) 1798–1870, md. Anna Maria Brosius, 1805–1892; Harrison (Harry) Rabuck, 1823–1861, md. Cath. K. Rebuck (his cousin), 1825–1904; Emanuel Rabuck, 1849–1918, md. Julie Ann Shade, 1851–1919; Anson Rabuck, 1877–1949, md. Sarah R. Klinger, 1886–1967; Mary S. Rabuck, 1910–2006, md. George M. Troutman, 1907–1976.

Pages 1 and 2 of Bonnie Lee Raybuck Jones family history follows:

1758 – Jan. 17th, Catherina Elieabetha Rehbock (in), a widow of Andreas Rehbock is now buried beside her husband. Catherina Elieabetha Rehbock age 68 years old. Bieber, Germany. Abstract from the Reformed Church Book dated 1724 to 785, Evangelical Church, Bieber Germany. Above: the parents of Valentine Rehbock, Catherina Elisabetha & Jh. Andreas Rehbock. Valentine Rehbock the pioneer ancestor of Northumberland County, Pa.

1757 – April 25th – Valentine Rehbock son of Andreas and Catharina Elisbetha Rehbock, a. yeoman of this place (Bieber) married Anna Barbara single daughter of Johann Georg Baldauf of (Röhrig).

1765 – Valentine Rehbock, a miner in Bieber, in the Principality of Hassen & Hanau, after a trial in Marburg, finding him guilty of encouraging people to emigrate to America, acting as an agent, left at the request of the government, and was granted permission to emigrate himself and family to America.

1765 – Sept. 9th – Valentine and family, (4 in the party) arrived in the port of Philadelphia, Penna. from Rotterdam & Cowes, by the ship called *Chance*. Valentine signed the Oath to the King, at the State House in Phila. 216 Whole Freights were consigned to Mr. Robert Ruecastle, paid the 26th of Sept. 1765. Valentine and his family may next be found in the Heidelberg Twp. area of then Berks Co. Penna. He may have served his indenture there; it was also the same area where relatives and friends are found on early records. Valentine and wife Anna Barbara. nee Balda(in), also their two sons born in Germany, 1st son Johann Heinrich, born. Feb. 20th 1758 in Bieber, & 2nd son Johann Adam born July 8th 1763, in Bieber, Germany, turned.to farming in Pa.

1769 – July 14th; son Johann Michael, was born in Heidelberg Twp. Berks Co. Penna.

25. 14 Hillside Drive, Pine Grove, Pennsylvania 17963.

1771 – Nov. 6th, son Johann Nicholas, was born, baptism record; listed at the Myerstown Tulpehocken Church of Christ, Lebanon Co. Penna. Noted on the record are the words; (from beyond the Blue Mountains), parents; Valentine & wife, :Barbara. Sponsors; Johann Nicholas Brosius & Barbara Hedrig, single, Leb. Co. Pa.

1772 – Northumberland Co. Penna. was formed, Augusta one of the original townships, located near the Berks Co. line, south of Line Mountain, was first settled by men & families from Berk Co. among them were Rehbock, Reitz, Hederich, Ferster, Schmidt, Brosius, and Schaffer.

1773 – May 11th, original patent to survey of 120 acres in Pine Grove Twp. to Valentine Rhebock of Berks Co. Pa. In 1771, Pine Grove Twp. Penna. (now Sch. Co.), divided from Bethel Twp. Berks Co. In 1797, Valentine Rehbock sold the land to Jacob Reiss, he in turn sold the land to a Zimmerman in 1821, deed Sch. Co. Pa. recorded.

1774 – Valentine Rehbock listed as married taxable of Augusta Twp. (later Mahanoy), Northumberland Co.; also as a family man and pioneer of the area south of Line Mt. near Upper Mahantongo, which is now presently in Sch. Co. Pa.

1774 – Sept. 21st, son Johann Peter was born, Northumberland Co. Baptized; Himmel's Ch. Nth. Co. Pa. Parents: Valentin & Barbara. Rebock, sponsor: Henrich Reitz, (single).

1776 – June 30th, Anna Barbara Rebock(in), was a communicant of the Himmel's Lutheran (Evangelical) Church, Nth. Co. Pa. (Note: the Rehbock's belonged to the Evangelical faith in Germany.)

1778 – Valentine Rebock listed as a taxable of Mahanoy Twp. a division of the original Augusta Twp., south of Line Mt., taken in 1775 of Northumberland Co. Penna.

1780 – May 20th, Bans are posted for Valentine's son Jh. Adam Rebock & Anna Maria nee Haubt, both age 17, then publicly confirmed and received into Himmel's Evangelical Ch.

1781 – Valentine Rebook, taxed for 100 acres & 1 horse, Mahanoy Twp. Nth. Co. Penna.

1781–1782 – Valentine Rehbock, is overseer of poor, of Mahanoy Twp. Nth. Co. Penna. 1782. Mrs. Barbara Rehbock, listed as a faithful communicant of Himmel Luth Evan. Ch. 1785 – Sept. 5th, Valentine Rebook taxed & deeded for 150 acres and 1 horse, Nth. Co. 1786 – Valentine Rebook is a Northumberland County Township Official.

1787 – Valentine Rebock owned & taxed for 170 acres & 1 horse, Nth. Co. Mahanoy Twp.

1789 – Valentine Rebook, Supervisor of Mahanoy Twp. a sub-division of Augusta Twp. Nth. Co. Penna.

1790 – Valentine Rehbock, (#192) Nth. Gb. 1 male 16 & up includes head of household, 4 males 16 & under, & l female listed in Pa. Head of Family and Census of 1790.

1797 – Valentine Rhebock sold his land of 120 acres in Pine Grove Twp. to Jacob Reiss.

1798 – Mar. 20th – By Commonwealth of Penna on deed by patent or grant to Valentine & Elias Rebook, the acreage later owned jointly by Valentine's sons; Jh. Adam and Jh. Michael Rebook located in Upper Mahanoy Twp. area of Nth. Co. Penna.

1800 – Census of Penna. Nth. Co. – Valentine Rehbock & wife are listed as both, age 45 & over, of Mahanoy Twp. (#286) – lm., 2m., 4f.

1800 – Last entry of Barbara Rebook, as Communicant of Himmel Luth. Evan. Ch. date Oct. 5th. Anna Barbara nee Balda Rehbock wife of Valentine Rehbock, to October 15, 1807?

1802 – May 19th – Letters of administration, (died interstate-without will), issue for estate to sons; Jh. Michael (adm.) and Jh. Adam Rebock, Nth. Co. Suretries; Leonard Reitz & George Brosius, neighbors & relation to sons, (Nth.Co. Court House), for Valentine Rehbock, ___ to ___.

Anna Barbara & Valentine Rebock's known children:[26]

1. Johann Heinrich: born Feb. 20th, 1758, at 5:00 P.M. – Bieber, Germany. Bapt. 21st. Sponsor: Johann Heinrich Georg from Rohrig.
2. Anna Catherina: born July 24th, 1760, at 5:00 P.M. – Bieber, Germany. Bapt. 26th. Sponsor: Anna Catherina Sach(in) from Lohrhaupten. Anna Catherina Rehbock died Oct. 2nd, 1762, at 7:00; buried the 3rd, age 2 y. & 10 wk.
3. Johann Adam: born July 8th, 1763, at 7:00 – Bieber, Germany. Bapt. 10th. Sponsor: Johann Adam Sensel, a single son of Balthasar Sensel, from the GaBe.
4. Johann Michael: born July 14th, 1769, at Heidelburg Twp. Berks Co. Penna.
5. Johann Nicholas: born Nov. 6th, 1771, at Pine Grove Twp. Berks Co. Penna.
6. Johann Peter: born Sept. 21st, 1774, at Nth. Co. Bapt. Oct. 4th at Himmel Church.

The Village of Bieber, Germany in the province of Hesse-Hanau. Three churches are within the village, Evangelical (Reformed) church, center, Catholic church to the left, and a Lutheran church is to the right, surrounded by trees.

26. The first three children were found in the Reformed Church Book 1724 to 1785 of the Evangelical Church Congregation, Bieber, Germany.

Evangelical-Reformed church in Beiber. This church was built seven years before Valentine emigrated to America. The church record books dated 1724-1785 indicate the formation of the church to be much older. The early church record books name the family members of Valentine Rehbock.

The Evangelical/Reformed Church in Beiber associated with the Valentine Rehbock Family.

A view of ancestral Rebuck home sites. Valentine Rehbock's pioneer home was located in the background of photo center. A log barn remained in 2019. An old Rebuck log house in the foreground, is lately recalled as the Vernon Rebuck residence. This is south of Greenbrier, SR 2007.

The Valentine Rehbock home site on Hunter's Junction Road. Only the log barn is seen here. The log house was lately removed. It stood photo center where the open green grass is seen.

The following photos courtesy of Carol Smeltz and Steve E. Troutman. Carol lived here in her younger years in the house which was located to the right of the barn.

Valentine Rebuck barn, Greenbrier, Pennsylvania, Township Road, Hunter's Junction.

The barn builders numbered each log joint. The wooden peg was placed in the drilled hole.

Valentine Rebuck barn log corner joints and carpenter's numerals. The logs were placed quite closely and beautifully morticed to stack in place on top of each other. Photos courtesy of Carol Smeltz. The timbers and boards were salvaged for reuse.

Village of Rebuck: Kehres's Store and Hotel

This community along the Schwaben Creek became a center of commerce and culture. Himmel's Church, the earliest established in this valley, is located nearby.

A Brief History of Himmel's Church

Himmel's Church was organized in 1773. A log building served the two congregations, Lutheran and Reformed, until the Stone Church was built in 1818. A high pulpit and a balcony were two interesting features of this building. Money left over from building this structure was spent on a pipe organ, which was installed shortly after 1818, being one of the first pipe organs in the area. This organ was in constant use until 1953.

Stone Church.

The first German Lutheran and Reformed settlers along the Schwaben Creek founded the church just four years after the Tulpehocken Road had been completed from Reading to the south side of the Mahanoy Mountain. In 1774 a land grant was issued by the colony of Pennsylvania, and a log church and log schoolhouse were built. The log schoolhouse is still standing, about 200 yards north of the present church building and until recently served as the sexton's house. Karl Henry Kauffman served as the first schoolmaster. The log school was used until 1870 when the public school system was adopted in Washington Township. The official church records were lost in the 1959 fire but a copy in the archives of the Northumberland County Historical Society in Sunbury indicates that it is the oldest church record in existence in Pennsylvania outside of Philadelphia. It was begun in 1776 by the Reverend John Michael Enterline and consists largely of baptismal and communicants' records. The first Lutheran Church Council consisted of J. Nicholas Brosius and Peter Ferster, deacons and Daniel Kobel and George Heim, elders. In 1780 the names of Andrew Ketterli and Peter Schmidt appear as officers of the Reformed congregation. The first baptisms were those of Johan and Maria Kobel on June 7, 1774, children of Henry and Catherine Kobel. The first communion was administered on June 30, 1776, to 64 persons, four days before the passage of the Declaration of Independence. From 1773 to 1847 Himmel's Church was part of the extensive Lykens Valley Charge. In 1847 it became part of the Mahanoy Parish, which was comprised of six congregations including Himmel's, Rebuck; Emmanuel, Hunter Station; David's, Hebe; St. Paul's, Urban; Zion, Herndon; and St. John's, located five miles east of Herndon. This Parish later included St. Peter's, Red Cross and existed into the 1960s when it was dissolved. The name Himmel's is unique in church nomenclature. Most early Lutheran and Reformed churches were named after a prominent family or biblical character. However, there is only one

Himmel's Church, which translated means Heaven's Church.

The need for larger facilities led to the building of the frame structure in 1903. Stained glass windows and a steeple reaching 105 feet into the sky made this building reverently beautiful. The one-room Sunday school aided the cause of Christian education over the years. This building was constructed almost entirely of timber and lumber harvested from the church-owned timberland, which, with the farmland, was part of the original land grant. The labor was furnished by the members. This was the building that was destroyed by fire.

The morning of January 18, 1959, was clear and cold, with the temperature dropping eight degrees below zero. At about 4:30 AM, several neighbors discovered that the church was on fire, but even then, the fire was beyond control. All we could do was watch as our church was destroyed by fire. The intense heat melted the altar brassware and much of the bell. The original record books, the old pipe organ, and the old pewter communion set were destroyed. The communion set currently in use was in the janitor's house and so was the only article not destroyed by the fire. An ominous stillness lay over the scene on Sunday as many came to see and left with saddened hearts.

But the good people of Himmel's Church would not let even such severe misfortune overcome them. A meeting was held on Monday evening to plan the recovery. The auditorium of the new Mahanoy Joint High School at Mandata was made available to us for worship services, and we happily accepted the offer. This was the prelude to many other offers of help. We shall be eternally grateful for all that we have received from others.

Himmel's Church, 1903–1959.

The Building Committee was organized on March 8th; Mr. Malcolm Clinger of Lewisburg was chosen as our architect on March 17th; representatives of the two Synods met with us and helped us in our planning for the new church. The final sketch was adopted in June by a congregational vote. Ground-breaking Service was held on March 20, 1960, with our architect, Mr. Clinger, the speaker. Work began and progressed rapidly, with the laying of the cornerstone on May 29th, the Reverend Ralph Robinson, Secretary of the Central Pennsylvania Synod, ULCA, as the guest speaker.

Anson Rabuck, (1877–1949), married Sarah R. Rabuck, (1886–1967). Sarah was a born Klinger& Great grandparents of Steve E. Troutman, grandparents of Earl G. Troutman. Earl was born in 1928 at the Anson Rabuck farm east of the Village of Erdman Photo by Earl G. Troutman.

Andreas Reitz homestead located between Greenbriar and the Himmels Church, recently an Everett farm. Conversation with Walter Reitz who lived all his life nearby the Himmels Church, provided this identification.

Fisher's Foundry, Rebuck, PA, photo by Steve E. Troutman in 1972. This industry produced the well known Fisher plow. The building had an overhead roller rail track to move products.

Spring 1911, in Rebuck, PA. Back team driver is John Treon. The horses are Bud and Tops. Front team driver is Morris Rebuck with James E. Rebuck on his lap. Adjacent on the seat is Frazer Schreffler. Standing are lda and Samuel Rebuck and Zimmey Feger of Leck Kill. Children are Katie (Rebuck) Crissinger, Samuel Rebuck, and Willaim (Schimmel) Rebuck

March 17, 1946, C.T. Reitz and wife married 43 years. Maurice Rebuck and wife married 46 years. Postcard F.L. Kehres and son, Rebuck, PA, 1910.

Threshing in Rebuck, PA. Steam traction engine with belt drive. Threshing machines were used to separate grain from the straw.

Pioneer cabin near Himmels Church. This building was located on a triangular piece of ground next to the Luther Rebuck-Reitz homestead.

Steve E. Troutman on the Mush Rebuck farm, in Rebuck, PA. He is standing in front of the Seven Sacred Circles. Steve Rebuck described the origin of the Seven Sacred Circles. Steve Rebuck had a genealogical connection to Native Americans in the Schwaben Creek Valley. These circles were characterized by vegetation growth differing from the adjoining natural field grasses. These circles had their origin with the Native Americans who established spiritual fires on this hillside. The resulting burned soil promoted the growth of unique grasses which grew as ground cover. For more information see the book Tulpehocken Trail Traces, p. 105, published by Sunbury Press.

The Reitz-Rebuck homestead photos are courtesy of Steve Rebuck, a life long resident of Rebuck.

Luther Rebuck farm. Sarah Rebuck, daughter of Luther Rebuck and Maria (Rebuck) Reb.uck. This original loghouse occupied by Rebuck and Reitz families in the pioneer days had an addition on the east side. This addition has been removed in the lower picture.

Joe E. Kehler's hotel was demolished by an explosion of acetylene gas. This gas was being generated from raw materials in the basement of the hotel. Acetylene gas was sold here for lighting purposes. The explosion blew the roof off the hotel. Boards can be seen hanging in the trees. This building stood north of the main Village of Rebuck. Photo courtesy of Lawrence Keim, from a newspaper describing the event.

Earl Marvin Drumheller, Interview, September 2024

Earl is a lifelong resident of the Schwaben Creek Valley. His first school experience was near the Village of Rebuck. The name of the school was Morning Star School. The school stood north of the Wesleyan Church which is located on Schwaben Creek Road. Morning Star, one-room school, burned down. Another school house was needed. Equity Hall, located west of Rebuck village, was chosen as the replacement for Morning Star. Equity Hall was established as a lodge hall and community grange. A public school was started on the upper floor of Equity Hall. Students climbed the stairway to the upstairs room which had a pot belly stove. Howard and Aunt Molly Wolfe lived downstairs. Earl's siblings Mark, Marion, Evelyn, and Nelma Drumheller attended here. Earl was born February 22, 1943, while his brothers were at this school. He was told by his mother that it was so warm on the day he was born that the students wore short sleeved shirts to school that day.

In those days, the Village of Rebuck included a garage, blacksmith shop, Kehres' General Store, and Drumheller's Hotel. John Kehres sold the store to Mr. Treon, and it burned down. "Windy" Schmeltz had a house and barn across the street from Drumheller's hotel. This house and barn were removed for road construction. Kehres' store burned in 1920 where the post office was located. Earl's grandfather, David Clark Drumheller, became the postmaster at Drumheller's hotel and store business. David was better known as D. C. David Clark Drumheller was the postmaster from 1920 to 1943. Earl's father, Marvin David Drumheller, became the postmaster in 1943. People referred to him as M. D. until the next generation took over. Earl Drumheller was appointed postmaster in 1975.

Drumheller's hotel was originally much smaller in size than it is now. A dance hall was added to the original building. This dance hall was first located on the south side of the main road, east of the former Crissinger garage. This hall, a large wooden structure, was moved across the street and around the back of the store where it was added to the Drumheller building. Jackson Brosius moved this building completely. Jackson was a carpenter and lived where Greg Erdman lives now in Greenbrier. This extraordinary move was completed in 1937 or 1938, with the aid of a motor truck. The building was pulled on rollers to its new foundation behind the hotel.

Earl attended Morning Light School after Equity Hall. This school was located on the farm where Merlin Francis Hoke and his wife, Vena (Erdman) Hoke located near Himmel's Church. The school building is now incorporated as part of this residence. Earl attended here three years. Annabelle Hillbush was his teacher. She married Clyde Adams. Earl had two years of public education at Union School. The school stood near the residence of Richard Adams on Schwaben Creek Road. It has been removed. Earl attended Red Cross School, as well. This was a two-room school, located in an empty field, along Route 225, near the location of Heim's Disposal. The building last served as an administrative office for the Line Mountain School District before its removal.

Earl remembers the existence of another barroom nearby Drumheller's. This business was located between Rebuck village and Himmel's Church. It was a small establishment, located next to the Schwaben Creek, which provided an additional opportunity for those seeking additional refreshment, after leaving Drumheller's!

Drumheller's Hotel, Rebuck, Pennsylvania

Drumheller's Hotel, residence, bar, restaurant, store, and post office in Rebuck.

A large sign in front of the hotel advertising "Consumer Discount Loans" is recalled. This was a business place for all the needs in the community. An attached dance hall, in the back, provided entertainment with local musicians. The barroom served food and beverages. Mr. Carta purchased the property with intentions of building apartments within this large complex.

Equity Hall, September 2024

International Order of Odd Fellows Lodge, Grange Hall, and one-room school. The current residents have decorated for Halloween. Ingelfritz is the owner of the dwelling.

The Mystery of Daniel Ferster's Death[27, 28]

Late summer of 1926, the Greenbrier area was stunned with the news of the discovery of a dead body on the Levi Ferster farm. The youngest son of Levi Ferster had his throat cut and his body had other cuts, scrapes, and bruises. Authorities, local police, and State Police were at odds as to the cause of his death.

This story created a mystery in several different ways. The first mystery, was it a homicide or was it a suicide? Why were police unable to get the cooperation of the residents when authorities questioned them? The coroner ruled it as a clear case of murder. The police maintained from the beginning the youth had no enemies and may have been thoroughly obsessed with his religious studies that he may have been temporarily deranged and decided to take his life. The mystery took five years before the whole story came to light.

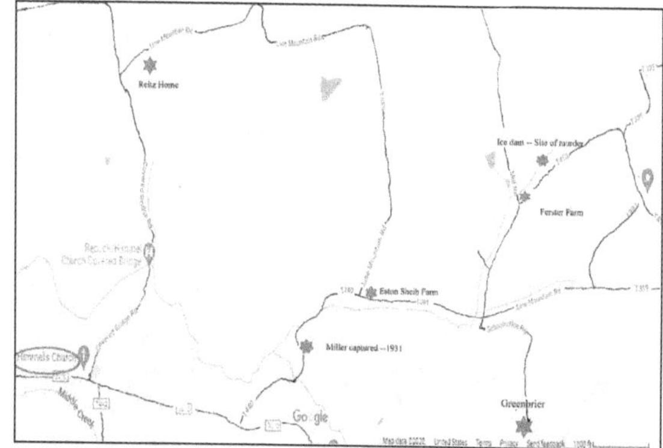

This area is between Himmel's Church and the Village of Greenbrier. Himmel's Church is circled lower left corner. Miller captured 1931, lower center of map. Greenbrier village, lower right. Eston Scheib farm map center. Ferster farm, middle right. Ice Dam, site of murder, north of Ferster farm.

Greenbrier is located approximately two miles east of the village of Rebuck. The population consisted primarily of Pennsylvania Germans, many of whom were offspring of the area's pioneers. Greenbrier had a combination post office and grocery store, a hardware store, several mills, and various small businesses. The community was close knit and many families attended close-by Himmel's Church. The community had a fraternal organization named the Greenbrier

27. Dale Reiner, of Dalmatia, is an active historical researcher. He has addressed many groups with his presentations of local history. Dale contributed the following narrative which was a presentation to the Northumberland County Historical Society in 2024.

28. The source of information for this story has been newspaper articles dated from 1926 and 1931. Police records and coroner records were not available. It would be interesting to read the reports the police and district attorney recorded and their reasoning to insist suicide was the cause of death.

Grange, which had a membership of 200; the Greenbrier Band with a membership of thirty-five; and a one-room school house, Brier Public School.

The Ferster name was well established in the Greenbrier area. Often referred to as Ferster's Valley, these families consisted of farmers, wheelwrights, carpenters, and other agricultural related fields. Levi Ferster married Mary Kahler and they had six children, with Daniel being the youngest. Daniel was a quiet young man, who engaged in activities and games with schoolmates, neighbors, and the youth at his church. He had a passion for hunting and raising and training his dogs.

Ferster Family Farm at the base of Line Mountain, now Donnie and Karen Kauffman's farm.

Daniel was a close student of the Bible and used his Sunday school to pursue his studies of the scripture. He attended church on a regular basis and lived a life above reproach, an example worth following. It may be, police say, that he was so thoroughly obsessed with his religious studies that he may have been temporarily deranged and decided to take his life. Moreover, prior to his death his friends had noticed that he had become depressed.

The death of Daniel Ferster took place close to the Ferster farm along Line Mountain in Washington Township. Newspaper reports from lower Northumberland County stated that authorities faced one of the most gruesome and baffling mysteries in many years following the discovery of the body of Daniel Ferster, 26, with his head almost severed, near Line Mountain, in Rebuck, about 600 yards from the Ferster home. Upon returning from the scene of the crime, Coroner J. K. Fisher, stated positively that it was a case of murder.

Saturday afternoon, September 4, Ferster, along with his two beagle dogs, left his home and headed for the mountain, intending to train the dogs for the coming hunting season. He assured his mother that he would return after the training session with the dogs. His words to his mother as he was leaving "I'm taking the dogs out for training. Don't worry!"

When he failed to appear on Saturday evening members of the family became alarmed and began a search of the immediate area. With no trace of the body having been found on Saturday evening, a group of men from the Rebuck section combed the entire hillside and mountains all day Sunday near the home. The search was continued on Sunday night, but again with no results.

Monday a general search was ordered and the county and state authorities notified. The search group was augmented by Boy Scouts from Sunbury. Monday evening, at about 6 o'clock William Ferster, a brother, and Wesley Snyder, a nephew, of the slain youth, came across the body in a clump of bushes not more than 600 yards from the family homestead. Authorities were immediately notified. Coroner Dr. J. K. Fisher went to the scene of the crime and investigated. The condition of the body and the surrounding section where it was found indicated conclusively that it was murder of the most brutal kind. The head of the Ferster body was almost severed with a sharp instrument. The right side of the neck had been slashed into the backbone and all the muscles and arteries in the neck had been cut. Both legs were badly bruised as was one arm and a large bruise mark was noticeable on the back.

The clump of bushes where the body was found was in a swampy section of the farm. A spring located close by provided a water supply to fill this small dam and supply the family with ice for spring and summer. Footprints in the mud were at wide intervals, indicating that the murderer ran from the scene. Marks of a scuffle near a large willow tree and blood stains were found. A large blood spot on the tree seemed to indicate to the authorities that the youth had been pushed against the tree and his throat cut while he was standing up. The body was cast into the bushes with the head almost severed, according to the county coroner. All the valuables in the young man's clothing, including his watch, were intact when the body was found, precluding any belief that robbery may have been the motive. A small knife, which members of the family failed to identify, was found near the scene of the murder, but authorities doubted that it was the instrument used by the murderer. It was too small, they believed, to inflict the wounds found in the youth's throat.

Persons living in that section told authorities they saw a small automobile parked near the scene of the murder and authorities attempted to learn the identity of the occupants with the hope that their information would reveal something tangible toward the solution of the mystery. The state trooper later reported they were still working to locate the phantom coupe which was seen near the scene of the murder. They reported they had not received any new leads.

State police working on the case to establish a motive for the death of Ferster indicated that valuable information was being withheld from them and that their investigation was being hampered. From the statements of Sergeant Kaufman, in charge of the Sunbury detail, it was concluded that several residents of that section were not telling all they knew in connection with the case. The investigation would continue until a solution or a motive was found.

County Detective Charles Densevich and the state police began investigating the idea that Ferster may have committed suicide. After four days, during which almost every adult inhabitant of the section was interviewed, the officials gave up the work to rest when Ferster was buried. They resumed their investigation the following day. Densevich said that it was his personal belief and that of the state police that Ferster tried first to end his life by hanging, using a dog chain thrown over the limb of the willow tree near the spot where his body was found. When he failed in this, he used a small knife to cut his throat, which was also found near the body. He then staggered away from the tree to a clump of bushes, where his lifeless body was found by his brother and his young nephew.

District Attorney Edward Raker also believed that it was a clear case of suicide. He had gathered evidence and could not see motive for murder. Every detail had been examined, and suicide seemed to be the only answer to the question. State police were also of this opinion. A bloodstained knife was found about seven feet from the dead man's body and was thoroughly examined. It was found that the smaller blade of the knife, which was about two inches long, was used.

There were no other marks on Ferster's body when it was found except the deep gash in his neck and bruises around his ankles. His clothes were not disarranged, and his money, watch, and other belongings were found in his clothes. He was not known to have any enemies in the neighborhood. Because of these reasons Mr. Raker was positive that Ferster was not murdered. This description by the District Attorney differed from that of the coroner's description of Ferster's body.

Ferster's family was steadfast in their opinion that he was murdered. Friends and relatives of the dead man had been questioned endlessly, but most of them remained silent. However, it was the opinion of the investigators that he committed suicide; whereas his immediate family stuck to the supposition that he was murdered.

A resident from the West Cameron area had dogs barking over a period of two nights, rounded them up, and returned them to the Ferster family.

A coroner's jury was organized, and this was followed by a later decision that Ferster was "killed by a person unknown to this jury" at the inquest conducted last week by Dr. Fisher, county coroner. The verdict stating that Ferster came to his death "by some unknown person cutting his throat," was meant to convey the conviction that the young man had been murdered despite the theory held by state and county authorities investigating the case that he took his own life. The action of the jury came after Coroner Fisher had outlined to the jury the result of his investigations which tended to show that Ferster had not died by his own hand. The jurors had previously heard the stories of Ferster's brother and nephew, who came up on the body. The small, rusty pocket knife found near the body could not have been used to inflict the wounds, he said. Moreover, the knife could not be identified as belonging to Ferster, and his own knife was found at home. The coroner further held that a willow tree, about 20 feet high, six or eight feet in diameter, about eighteen feet from the spot where the body was found. He found clotted blood and hair on the bark of the tree. He expressed the theory that the young man had been held against the willow tree while his throat was slashed. Torn clothing, cuts on the forehead and nose, bruises on both hands, arm, and legs, and a large bruise on the back indicated foul play, he said, as did the beaten down condition of the bushes in the vicinity and the numerous footprints. Some of the latter led through the newly plowed soil and apparently were those of a person running. The fact that Ferster's hat was found 500 yards away from the spot where his body lay and that his hunting dogs, his most faithful companions, had left the scene and were found some distance away also precluded the suicide theory, he held. Furthermore, no motive of any kind could be advanced for suicide, the jury was told. The case was quite comprehensively reviewed and because there were no witnesses save William Ferster and William Snyder and their testimony had already been heard, there was nothing for the jury to consider but a general resume of the case. Whether or not the action of the coroner's jury had any bearing upon the activities of the state police and county authorities at work on the case was not indicated. The jury was composed of C. P. Kauffman, D. W. Bordner, and G. W. Reitz of Washington Township; William Forney, William Lentz, and C. J. Reitz of Sunbury.

In December 1926, Northumberland County Commissioners and Levi Ferster each offered a reward of $500 for the arrest and conviction of the murderer of Daniel Ferster. At this point the investigation was suspended until any new evidence surfaced.

Almost five years had passed since the mystery death of Levi Ferster. Police had not published any new information on the case. The Greenbrier area returned to its quiet and serene lifestyle. But that was all about to change.

On June 15, 1931, a highway robbery occurred on the road leading from Gown City to Trevorton. The daring holdup occurred when a bandit pulled a weapon from his coat pocket while standing in the middle of the road. He fired a shot into the windshield just missing the driver. James Smith was not struck by the shot, but glass from the shattered windshield did cut him. The bandit stole seven dollars from Smith and fled the scene.

George L. Miller, Shamokin, was arrested four days later. After a police grilling, he confessed to the robbery of the bakery truck and firing a shot through the windshield. Miller, who was middle-aged and crippled, was arrested and formally charged with the holdup of Smith on Monday morning. Miller offered to take police to the location where he disposed of the weapon.

Miller led police to the Lower Road of West Cameron, which runs along the Mahanoy Creek to Hunter Station. It was along this creek that Miller pointed to the spot where he threw the weapon. As the officers walked around searching, Miller slipped away into the heavy thicketed woodlands and mountainous terrain. Miller knew every inch of ground and every trail. Police continued their search and they learned Miller came down from mountain Saturday night to forage for food at the home of his brother-in-law Emanuel Reitz. Police searched the area, but Miller was gone. He did leave a note addressed to his two nephews: "Walter or Harry, see that Anne gets this money." Walter and Harry were the sons of Emanuel. The last will and testament of Miller was written with a bullet whittled to a sharp point. The bullet was found in Miller's pocket and troopers knew immediately the purpose of the object.

Expecting another visit, two State Troopers hid in the Reitz basement the following night. After several hours' vigil, they heard a prowler. It was Miller, hungrier than ever and looking like a wild man who was being driven to desperation.

Miller opened fire and officers returned with a salvo of shots. Miller dropped to the ground, rolled over a couple times, and rolled over an embankment. He lay motionless and apparently dead.

When the police went over to the edge of the embankment, Miller opened fire, grazing one of the officers. A battle ensued and Miller slid away to safety. The officers picked up his trail, following blood stains as much as possible, but Miller, familiar with the territory, escaped.

State troopers thoroughly searched the neighborhood of the Reitz farm and that proved fruitless. The search spread out and then, when passing a farmhouse, a young girl motioned to the officers. She said she saw a man cross the road into a field.

The officers abandoned the vehicle and moved closer when they suddenly saw the man trying to conceal himself behind a tree. One of the officers called out to Miller to give himself up. Miller's reply was a shot just missing the officer. The troopers returned Miller's fire, with several striking Miller. Miller worked his way to the head of a ridge which gave him a view of the troopers below, who then split up and gained an advantage. Miller was seen to go to his knees, and he made a desperate effort to crawl away, but the troopers reached the mortally wounded man just a moment before he died. Miller did not utter a word throughout the gun battle. The officers examined his body and found he had been wounded seven times.

The corner was called and he ordered the body removed to the undertaking establishment of C.P. Schaffer at Mandata. Miller's body was placed on the back of a small truck and was paraded throughout the area to assure the public the desperado had been captured.

Miller, 55, was a one-legged Shamokin garage mechanic, and alleged confessed bandit. Police indicated that the man was suspected of a long list of robberies and holdups. Victims feared reporting the incidents to authorities because of Miller's temper and his threats to shoot them and their family members. Many families were either related to him or knew him personally. He was an avid hunter and had acquired high skill with fire arms.

Funeral Director Charles Shaffer, from whose parlor the funeral of Miller was held, called for state police protection shortly before the service, fearing Miller's relatives would cause trouble. One guest openly made threats that he would "get even" with state police for slaying Miller. Threats were also made to some of the farmers and residents who assisted police in their search for Miller. It was also noted, Mrs. Annie Miller, widow of the slain bandit and who refused to accept the body, had attended the funeral.

The Reverend Hanning, pastor of the Gratz Lutheran Church, officiated the service and burial was at the Miller family plot at Gratz. In refusing to accept the body of Miller and thus become responsible for the funeral expenses, the Miller family let it be known that it was without funds. As residents of the city of Shamokin, they would have been called upon to bear a portion of the burial expenses. Some members of the family agreed to contribute to the expense.

The death mystery, which had baffled police for the past five years, was cleared up with the capture of Miller. According to the information now released by his death, he killed Ferster during an argument in a meadow near the Ferster home. The youth was beaten and his throat was cut. It was recalled that the body of Ferster was found in the meadow by his brother and nephew. As a result, the stigma of suicide upon the memory of Daniel Ferster had been removed when it was revealed that Miller was the killer. Miller killed Ferster during a quarrel over hunting dogs. These dogs were prized by Ferster and were well trained.

Close relatives knew from the outset that it was Miller who had done the killing, but their lips were sealed due to threats of death if they should reveal the facts. Dr. J. K. Fisher, county coroner, held to a theory of murder at the time and asked for a thorough investigation. There was little inclination on the part of other authorities to act in the case, however, and the supposition grew that it was a case of suicide, although no motive for such an act could be found.

Will and Daniel Ferster and their hunting dogs.

It was declared by neighbors of the Ferster family that Miller had been suspected of the killing from the start but in the absence of definite information and the laxity of police, nothing was ever done in the matter.

Morning Light One-Room School

This school was located in Washington Township on Middle Creek near Himmel's Church. It was the residence of the Merlin Hoch family for many years. The schoolhouse is currently a residence neighboring Dennis Kieffer. Charles Kline was the teacher pictured on the front cover of this souvenir booklet dated 1908. The souvenir booklet on the next page dated 1910 is also from Morning Light School. The teacher was

Morning Light School class of 1924. Photo courtesy of Gayle (Paul) Rebuck. Gertie Kieffer is Gayle Rebuck's maternal grandmother. She is in the third row, standing, wearing a white dress with a dark collar. Gertie's brothers are in the picture also. Clarence Kieffer is in the first row, second from the left. Lloyd Kieffer is in the first row, fourth from the left.

Morning Light School remodeled as a residence, Middle Creek Rd., Washington Twp.

John Hetrick. Katie Troutman is named as a student on all three booklets. She collected these booklets given by her teacher. These mementoes are courtesy of Walker Marks, Downingtown, Pennsylvania. His grandmother was Katie Troutman.

MORNING LIGHT

PUBLIC SCHOOL

District No. 4

Washington Twp., Northumberland Co., Pennsylvania

CHARLES KLINE, Teacher

School Board

Isaac Rebuck — Charles Brorius
James Rose, Treas.
Daniel Rothermel
George Lenker, Sec. — Elias Kobel, Pres.

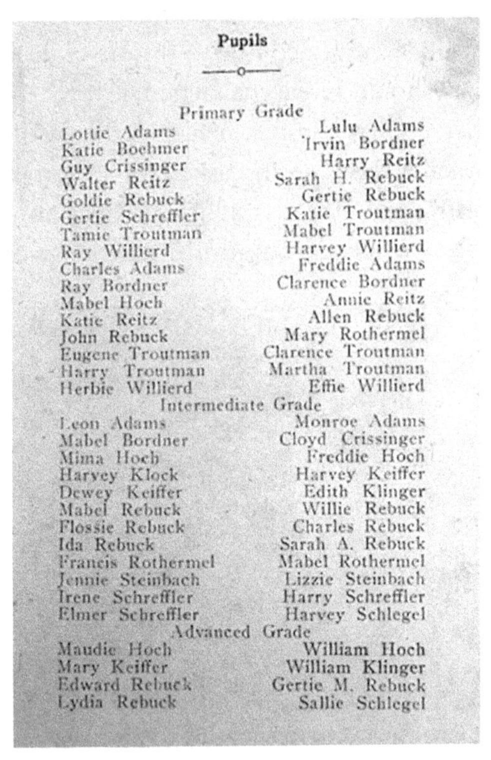

Pupils

Primary Grade	
Lottie Adams	Lulu Adams
Katie Boehmer	Irvin Bordner
Guy Crissinger	Harry Reitz
Walter Reitz	Sarah H. Rebuck
Goldie Rebuck	Gertie Rebuck
Gertie Schreffler	Katie Troutman
Tamie Troutman	Mabel Troutman
Ray Willierd	Harvey Willierd
Charles Adams	Freddie Adams
Ray Bordner	Clarence Bordner
Mabel Hoch	Annie Reitz
Katie Reitz	Allen Rebuck
John Rebuck	Mary Rothermel
Eugene Troutman	Clarence Troutman
Harry Troutman	Martha Troutman
Herbie Willierd	Effie Willierd
Intermediate Grade	
Leon Adams	Monroe Adams
Mabel Bordner	Cloyd Crissinger
Mima Hoch	Freddie Hoch
Harvey Klock	Harvey Keiffer
Dewey Keiffer	Edith Klinger
Mabel Rebuck	Willie Rebuck
Flossie Rebuck	Charles Rebuck
Ida Rebuck	Sarah A. Rebuck
Francis Rothermel	Mabel Rothermel
Jennie Steinbach	Lizzie Steinbach
Irene Schreffler	Harry Schreffler
Elmer Schreffler	Harvey Schlegel
Advanced Grade	
Maudie Hoch	William Hoch
Mary Keiffer	William Klinger
Edward Rebuck	Gertie M. Rebuck
Lydia Rebuck	Sallie Schlegel

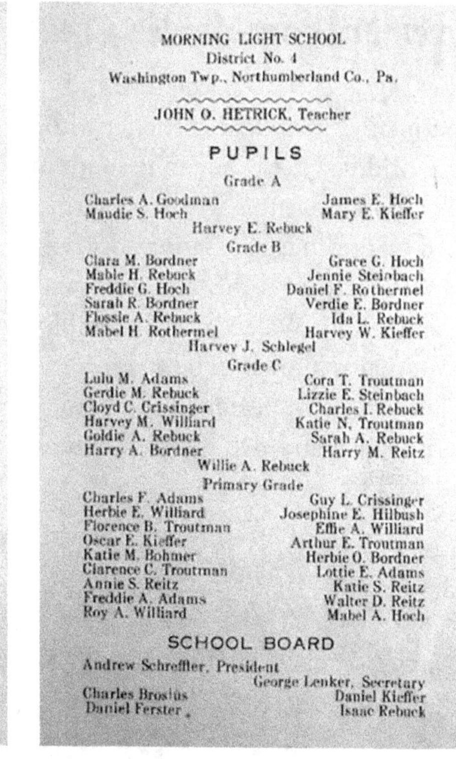

MORNING LIGHT SCHOOL
District No. 4
Washington Twp., Northumberland Co., Pa.

JOHN O. HETRICK, Teacher

PUPILS

Grade A

Charles A. Goodman	James E. Hoch
Maudie S. Hoch	Mary E. Kieffer
Harvey E. Rebuck	

Grade B

Clara M. Bordner	Grace G. Hoch
Mable H. Rebuck	Jennie Steinbach
Freddie G. Hoch	Daniel F. Rothermel
Sarah R. Bordner	Verdie E. Bordner
Flossie A. Rebuck	Ida L. Rebuck
Mabel H. Rothermel	Harvey W. Kieffer
Harvey J. Schlegel	

Grade C

Lulu M. Adams	Cora T. Troutman
Gerdie M. Rebuck	Lizzie E. Steinbach
Cloyd C. Crissinger	Charles I. Rebuck
Harvey M. Williard	Katie N. Troutman
Goldie A. Rebuck	Sarah A. Rebuck
Harry A. Bordner	Harry M. Reitz
Willie A. Rebuck	

Primary Grade

Charles F. Adams	Guy L. Crissinger
Herbie E. Williard	Josephine E. Hilbush
Florence B. Troutman	Effie A. Williard
Oscar E. Kieffer	Arthur E. Troutman
Katie M. Bohmer	Herbie O. Bordner
Clarence C. Troutman	Lottie E. Adams
Annie S. Reitz	Katie S. Reitz
Freddie A. Adams	Walter D. Reitz
Roy A. Williard	Mabel A. Hoch

SCHOOL BOARD

Andrew Schreffler, President
George Lenker, Secretary

Charles Brosius	Daniel Kieffer
Daniel Ferster	Isaac Rebuck

Pupils

Primary Grade

Lottie Adams	Lulu Adams
Katie Boehmer	Irvin Bordner
Guy Crissinger	Harry Reitz
Walter Reitz	Sarah H. Rebuck
Goldie Rebuck	Gertie Rebuck
Gertie Schreffler	Katie Troutman
Tamie Troutman	Mabel Troutman
Ray Willierd	Harvey Willierd
Charles Adams	Freddie Adams
Ray Bordner	Clarence Bordner
Mabel Hoch	Annie Reitz
Katie Reitz	Allen Rebuck
John Rebuck	Mary Rothermel
Eugene Troutman	Clarence Troutman
Harry Troutman	Martha Troutman
Herbie Willierd	Effie Willierd

Intermediate Grade

Leon Adams	Monroe Adams
Mabel Bordner	Cloyd Crissinger
Mima Hoch	Freddie Hoch
Harvey Klock	Harvey Keiffer
Dewey Keiffer	Edith Klinger
Mabel Rebuck	Willie Rebuck
Flossie Rebuck	Charles Rebuck
Ida Rebuck	Sarah A. Rebuck
Francis Rothermel	Mabel Rothermel
Jennie Steinbach	Lizzie Steinbach
Irene Schreffler	Harry Schreffler
Elmer Schreffler	Harvey Schlegel

Advanced Grade

Maudie Hoch	William Hoch
Mary Keiffer	William Klinger
Edward Rebuck	Gertie M. Rebuck
Lydia Rebuck	Sallie Schlegel

A Clover Mill on Middle Creek

On Labor Day weekend 2025, Steve and Joan Troutman visited Dennis Kieffer who lives along Middle Creek, one mile south of Himmel's Church. Dennis recalls his farm was owned by previous generations of Kieffers. At a very early date, the land was owned by the Heim family. We examined a building on his farm that is known to be a clover mill. The building has an appearance of a farm house with a cellar and two floors of living space and an attic.

Dennis Kieffer gave us a tour of the old clover mill. We used the cellar entrance closest to Dennis.

The walk-in cellar has a very high ceiling. The building was designed to allow water to flow through the cellar. An archway in the building foundation on the east side enabled water to enter the cellar. The flow of water then exited the cellar through the stone foundation wall. The water exit is not visible as this part of the cellar was remodeled to accommodate the storage of potatoes. The building rests on a stone foundation with the walls being at least twelve feet high on all four sides. The cellar floor is not level. A portion of the south cellar space is much lower than the rest of the cellar. There are four steps leading down to the stone arch, which is approximately three feet high. The arch is built of hand cut stones. The water wheel which powered the mill may have been located here in the lowest part of the cellar.

The stone arch for the mill race is inside the clover mill. A cement pad supporting a pump and water tank was later added to occupy a portion of the old waterway. The wooden steps provided access to the water pump. It is probable that this was the location of the water wheel which powered the clover mill. An under shot water wheel may have been used. This type of water wheel is turned by the flow of the mill race water, flowing underneath and against the wheel. An over shot water wheel rotates as the mill race water fills the pockets in the wheel from the top.

The cellar space is very spacious, compared to most old house basements. The very tall wooden steps accentuate the high ceiling. The stone walls have been plastered and white washed. Dennis said the cider barrel is empty.

A Northumberland County map of 1858 shows Washington Township. J. Kieffer is identified as the land owner to the east of the mill. This map identifies the clover mill location. The map locates the mill race leading to the clover mill. The mill race originated on Middle Creek, south of J. Kieffer's residence. A dam on Middle Creek provided the headwater which flowed through the mill race, across the lowland, to the clover mill. From the mill a tail race carried the water back to Middle Creek several hundred feet downstream from the mill. This tail race construction is very unusual because the waterway was covered creating a stone arch tunnel. Dennis suggested the mill race was covered in the lowland fields to farm over it.

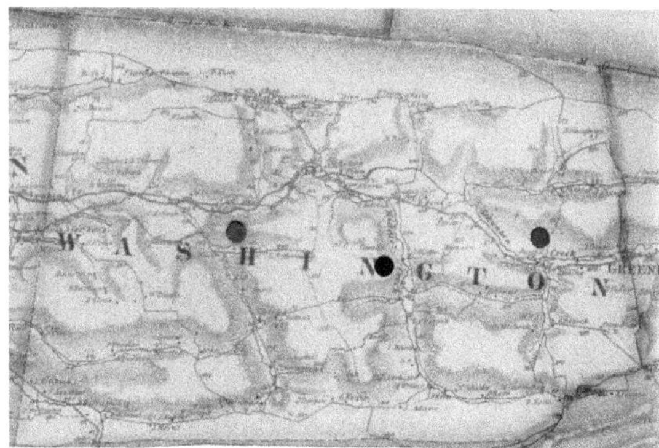

1858 Map of Washington Township, Northumberland County. The Kieffer's Middle Creek clover mill is in the center of the township. A clover mill is also located in the Village of Greenbrier and a fulling mill is located further to the west.

Red clover is known as a green manure crop. Before the development of commercial fertilizers, clover was commonly used in a rotation system to prepare fields for later crops of wheat, corn, or other grains. Clover mills were developed to collect and clean the seed. The early mills utilized rough cut millstones that crushed the flower heads between them as they rotated. The millstones were carefully leveled and placed just far enough apart to perform this operation without injuring the seed. The seed was expelled out the sides where it was collected. A fanning mill was then used to clean the seeds of chaff. It utilized a series of sieves of decreasing sizes

Dennis Kieffer and Joan Troutman stand where the old mill race was located. The mill race has been filled in. The mill race water flowed where green grass grows in front of the summer house. The water entered the race to the south where a dam was built across Middle Creek. The flowing water entered the cellar clover mill location through an arch in the house foundation. The water left the mill via the tale race which extended from this building across the lowland back to the Middle Creek. The Middle Creek flows south to north in the direction of the Himmel's Church.

that were mechanically shaken to screen out the larger material. Rotating fan blades created a breeze to blow away the light weight chaff and dust. Many early clover mills were water powered. The millstones would have measured only 18 inches in diameter, much smaller than those used in grist mills.[29]

Wesleyan Church near Rebuck

Wesleyan Church in 2024.

Anglican minister John Wesley (1703-1791) founded the Wesleyan Church in America. He was born in Great Britain, the son of Samuel Wesley, who was also a minister. John became the leader of the Evangelical Revival and founder of the Methodist Church in Great Britain and America.[30]

The Wesleyan Church in Rebuck is now renamed as "The Hub." The church is well known as a charitable organization.

A Fulling Mill on the Schwaben Creek

Northumberland County Maps dated 1858 and 1875 identify the location of a fulling mill between Rebuck and Red Cross. The Zook masonry business and residence is presently located nearby. This mill was situated in the lowland south of the Zook residence. The Schwaben Creek adjoins the mill location. According to the maps, a waterway from the creek led to the mill buildings.

A fulling mill processes wool into a form that allows thread to be produced. Fulling is a step in woolen cloth production which involves the cleansing of woven cloth (particularly wool) to eliminate lanolin, oils, dirt, and other impurities, and to make it shrink by friction and pressure. Fuller's earth is used as a part of this process.

There is a tradition of wool industry in the Schwaben Creek Valley. William Atkins established a woolen mill near Jacob's (Howerter's) Lutheran and Reformed Church further east on Little Mahantongo Creek. Hats and dyed clothing were made. The legend of Mae Paul, the shepherdess and the werewolf, attests to the husbandry of sheep in the Leck Kill area. The earliest cloth in the valley was made from linen derived from the flax plant. As later generations of residents obtained sheep, the use of woolen clothes soon followed.

Another mill in this area noted on the 1858 map, is a clover mill on Middle Creek. Middle Creek flows into the Schwaben Creek south of Himmel's Church. Dennis Kieffer's farm is presently near the location

29. The Mansfield Historical Society of Mansfield, Connecticut, describes the use and function of clover mills in its newsletter, Vol. 49, No.1, April 2013.

30. *World Book Encyclopedia.*

of this clover mill. A clover mill separates the clover seeds from the flower heads and chaff, by use of a mill stone.

Schwaben Creek American Indian Heritage

On a sunny afternoon in March of 2025, we traveled to the Schwaben Creek Valley in search of information about Native Americans. Steve Rebuck, now deceased, introduced this topic to me several years ago. It prompted a visit to his mother, Bobbi Maurer Rebuck. This encounter provided the necessary information to include in our book *Tulpehocken Trail Traces*,[31] describing the intermarriage of Native Americans and early settlers.

Steve Rebuck spoke of Moslock-Muschlock as the last dwelling place of Indian refugees in the Schwaben Creek Valley. We were hoping to find this place of encampment which Steve described to me in prior years. We traveled west down the Schwaben Creek Valley to the Rahn Troutman residence and food service business. We turned north at the intersection with Latsha Road. At the top of the hill is the Latsha farm. We traveled west on Picnic Road from the Latsha homestead farm and followed a narrow ground field road barely wide enough for one vehicle. We passed a picnic pavilion for which the road was named. We passed through an intersection and continued in a westerly direction on Picnic Road. A pick-up was approaching from the west. I stopped and hoped the truck would take to the field and allow us to pass. As we met, on the top of a high hill, I turned down my window and asked the driver if he knew where the encampment was that Steve Rebuck had told me about many years ago. The driver knew me and said, "Steve you are now at that encampment site."

Glen Kieffer was the pick-up driver. He is the farmer and landowner of the encampment site at this location. How very special our meeting place was! We met at the exact location at the right time. This was not a coincidence, but divine intervention. Glen pointed to the location of the dwelling place of Native Americans on his grandfather's farm in Washington Township. This spot was where I met Glen on Picnic Road. The location is within sight of his grandfather's farm in Cherrytown. The encampment was high on the side of a hill, south of Samuel Kieffer's farm in the valley below. This hillside location is flanked by small hollows on the east and on the west. Both have running water. A portion of the north facing hillside contains a small area, rather flat in topography. This flat terrace is where the Indian longhouse was established. Since the house was set on the ground, it had a ground floor. There was no stone foundation.

Some of the Kieffers of the Schwaben Creek Valley are grain farmers. Glen Kieffer's

31. Available from Sunbury Press.

family tree roots are deep in the soil of Washington Township. Glen Kieffer of Red Cross has a grandfather, Samuel Kieffer, who lived west of the Village of Rebuck on Route 49024. Samuel's farm is located at the base of Line Mountain. This area is known locally as Cherrytown. Glen farms the fields south of the old Kieffer homestead, where a home site was occupied by Seneca refugee Indians. The Long brothers from the Mahanoy Creek Valley have Seneca Indian ancestry through a Seneca woman originally from New York state. The Long brothers told Glen Kieffer about the exact location of the refugee encampment on his grandfather Samuel's farm. Steve Rebuck confirmed this location as well.

Glen Kieffer's lineage of Indian ancestry is traced to his mother. She was born a Peifer, grandmother Kehres, great grandmother Hetrick, great-great grandmother Gonsar, who was an Indian maiden. Glen Kieffer and Steve Rebuck shared a common ancestry with this Gonsar Indian princess from the Mahanoy Creek Valley. Steve Rebuck confirmed his genealogy which also included a great grandmother, Catherine Shade. She was Native American, originally from the Rebuck area.[32]

The Rebuck family is descended from Valentine Rehbock, the immigrant pioneer ancestor who settled north of Greenbrier at the early date of 1774. Valentine is listed as married and taxable in what was then Augusta Township, Northumberland County. In 1778 Valentine is listed as taxable in Mahanoy Township, a division of the original Augusta Township located south of the Line Mountain. Rebuck descendants populated the Schwaben Creek Valley and had knowledge of the earlier Native Americans. Steve Rebuck's great grandmother's diary was found in the Rebuck farm house attic. It included entries describing Native American places of spiritual worship. Seven sacred circles are identified as located on their Rebuck farm. These seven sacred circles were visible on the hillside south of James (Mush) Rebuck's farm.[33]

Steve Rebuck's great grandmother's diary also referenced the location of one of the last Indian encampments on the Moslock farm located north of the James (Mush) Rebuck farm. The diary stated that a camp was located on the corner of the Moslock farm. A fence row exists today marking the farm boundary. The camp was west of this fence row. Picnic Road leads to this fence row. The Moslock farm is presently Amish-owned.

Steve Rebuck recalled the annual Latsha family reunions at Himmel's Church. Steve Rebuck's great-grandmother came from the Latsha farm in Washington Township. There was often conversation with reference to relatives of Indian descent. Some of these names included Troutman, intermarried with a great-grandmother named Goodman, who was half Indian. *Bell's History of Northumberland County* lists George Goodman as serving in the War of 1812[34] with other familiar Mahantongo names. Nathan Goodman (1832-1910) and Sara are buried at David's Cemetery in Hebe.

These Troutman/Goodman people, relatives of Percy Troutman, were the last to live in the Dornsife kettle. A dwelling foundation

32. For more information describing this Maurer/Shade intermarriage see the book *Tulpehocken Trail Traces.*

33. See the book *Tulpehocken Trail Traces* for more information about the spiritual fires attended here by the Indians.

34. Pg. 395.

and a wall of stone remain there, north of Dornsife. Glen recalled the legend that gunpowder was manufactured in the Dornsife kettle, and a stone quarry site is visible on the north rim. Dynamite was used to blast the rock loose, which was used in building the stone piers for the Trevorton, Mahanoy, Susquehanna Rail Road Bridge, connecting Herndon to Port Trevorton.[35]

The Long brothers from the Mahanoy Valley are related to Steve Rebuck and the Latshas. They attended the Latsha Reunion as well. The Latsha Family homestead is on top of the hill above Rahn Troutman's residence. These Latshas also have Indian blood in their family tree. Nevin Latsha became a well-known owner/operator of a poultry growing and processing firm Mandata Poultry, located between Red Cross and Mandata.

Mandata was named for an Indian maiden who lived on the village site. The poultry plant was one of the area's largest employers in its time. An Indian maiden's picture was part of the company logo. Glen Kieffer suggested it was very appropriate, considering the Latsha's Indian heritage. Troy Latsha, son of Delroy Latsha, acknowledged the existence of Indian blood in the family. Steve Rebuck, now deceased, also confirmed the connection between the Latshas and American Indians.

The Bordner family of Red Cross lived next door to Glen Kieffer, south of Red Cross. Guy Bordner's wife, Jean Yohe, claimed Indian ancestry through the Gottshalls of the Mahanoy Valley. Glen Kieffer interviewed Jean (Yohe) Bordner in June of 2025. Jean is presently 96 years old and recalls past events accurately. She was one of 17 children raised on the farm where she still resides. Jean married Guy Bordner, and her homestead farm later became known as the Guy Bordner farm. It is located south of the Red Cross church. Jeans' great-grandmother, on her mother's side, had an Indian blood connection through the Yohe family name. Unfortunately, the born name of this great-grandmother is not known. Attempts to identify her Indian ancestry by name were made. Research in Harrisburg by the Bordner family determined that pertinent documents concerning this American Indian connection were destroyed in a fire in Harrisburg. It has been confirmed that this Indian princess married Benjamin Gottshall. The Gottshalls lived in the Cameron Valley along the Mahanoy Creek. They are identified on early maps, locating the Gottshall land ownership. The Gottshall family is credited with donating the ground to build a church in the Cameron Valley.

The following Indian heritage (names in italics) are from the Mahanoy Valley. These include Rebuck, Kieffer, Long, associated with *Gonsar*; Rebuck, Maurer, associated with *Shade*; and Troutman, associated with *Goodman*. The Mahanoy was referred to as the Cameron Valley during the coal mining industry. William Cameron was a wealthy landowner who developed underground coal mines in Lavelle, Helfenstine, Doutyville, and Gowen City. Cameron Township is his heritage. Hunter Station and Dornsife are also situated on the Mahanoy Creek in Little Mahanoy Township.

35. See the book published by Sunbury Press, *The Trevorton, Mahanoy, Susquehanna Railroad and Susquehanna River Bridge at Herndon.*

The Schwaben Creek Valley was part of the lands purchased by the Penn family through the Treaty of 1749. The Mahanoy Creek Valley was purchased from the Indians by the Penn family through the treaty of 1768. This was 19 years after the Treaty of 1749. Line Mountain was the boundary between the land purchases. The encroaching settlements of new land owners within the purchase of 1749 forced the Native Americans across Line Mountain to the unpurchased land of the Mahanoy Valley. Native Americans congregated in the Mahanoy Valley after the Indian Purchase of 1749. As the Indian clans migrated away from the Schwaben Creek Valley, some individuals were left behind. These people, separated from their family groups, experienced difficulty in obtaining the basic necessities of life. Steve Rebuck described them as refugees. Some Native Americans befriended early pioneers for food and sustenance. Some Indians intermarried with the white settlers and remained in the Mahantongo Valley.

March 23, 2025, Glen Kieffer poses on Picnic Road, Washington Township, Northumberland County. A Seneca Indian encampment of Native American refugees was situated behind Glen on the hillside below the road. This site was identified by members of the Long family and Steve Rebuck. The Moslock encampment site is located one-quarter mile west of the above location. Its location was identified in a diary kept by Steve Rebuck's great-grandmother. Glen Kieffer said there were two separate places of encampment in this vicinity. Line Mountain, seen in the background, was the established boundary between the Penn Family Indian purchases of 1749, which included the Mahantongo Valley and the Indian purchase of 1768, which included the Mahanoy Valley.

Troutman's Feed & Grain to Troutman's Food Service[36]

In the 1940s, Percy and Pauline Troutman ventured into the feed and grain business, providing bagged and bulk feed products to the area's farmers. With the help of Percy's brother, Derl, they would truck feed out of Baltimore and Lancaster. They began storing products in a small barn that was located on Slutter Valley Road, adjacent to their family farm. As the business grew, they quickly outgrew the neighboring barn. At the second location on Ferster Valley Road and State Route 225, Percy and Pauline Troutman started housekeeping directly across the street from the second storage location. During the 1950s, with a growing family and a growing business, they started looking for a location to settle down and expand their feed business.

A location became available from Merlin and Pauline Rebuck on Schwaben Creek Road, neighboring the Rebuck Farms between Taylor and Slutter Valley Roads. As construction of the new Troutman's Feed & Grain building-began, so did the construction of the new Himmel's Church following a devastating fire in January 1959. A total of

36. Author: Rahn Troutman. Editor: Kaitlyn Troutman.

1,400 dump truck loads of fill were hauled from Himmel's Church to the new Troutman property, with Percy Troutman providing a dump truck and Pat Latsha operating an excavating company. After the completion of construction, the feed mill opened in December 1960. The building, commonly known as The Mill, was the new home of Troutman's Feed & Grain. The building consisted of a showroom which offered a full complement of feeds, seeds, all farm needs, hardware, poultry equipment and a variety of animal drugs, medicines, and remedies. Also, within the building was an office, a large warehouse with a wooden tongue and groove floor, a grain elevator with five 15-ton grain bins, a back-in bay for the mobile feed grinder, and four large bays on the lower level. Troutman's Feed & Grain was a Wayne Feed Distributor.

In 1967, many changes were happening in the feed industry. Larger feed companies were contracting with large-scale chicken and hog facilities, which meant they were providing the feed and grain needed in their operations, leading to a decline in the mom-and-pop family farms. At that time, Troutman's entered into a merger with M.G. Henninger & Sons from Berrysburg.

Troutman's Feed & Grain Mill still operated until 1974, selling feed products. During these years, Percy worked at Henninger's in the office while Pauline worked at the Dornsife location, along with raising their six children: Patricia, Debra, Richard, Rahn, Bonita, and Angela.

While working at Henninger's, Percy learned of a French-fry business, known as D & D Fries, with owners, Ray Dockey and Ralph Daniels, who were ready to retire. This sparked an interest in the Troutmans, and they decided to take over the business in 1973. What started with a potato peeler, a few French-fry cutters, fryers, a 1964 Rambler Station Wagon, and a canvas tent has turned into three generations of the Troutman family making fresh-cut French fries. With Percy's son Rahn as the current proprietor, and the help of his wife, Traci, and their three children, Kaitlyn, Connor, and Kylie, the business has grown into a wholesale potato processing center, three mobile food concession trailers, and on-site catering, all based at the Schwaben Creek location. The Troutman's Feed & Grain Mill was transformed into Troutman's Food Service's home for bulk storage, catering supplies, potato processing equipment and storage, and the large bays storing the three mobile trailers, while still lovingly keeping the nickname The Mill. The Troutmans also became involved with the Pennsylvania Co-Operative Potato Growers booths at the Pennsylvania State Farm Show since January 1973. The entire booth, from all the cooking equipment, ventilation hoods, counters, and all other supplies are also stored at The Mill. Troutman's Food Service receives its potatoes from local farmers in the area, specifically from Red Hill Farms and Zimmerman Farms, both located in Pitman.

Lower Northumberland County has been home to all of the Troutman ancestors, but the last five generations have especially called the Schwaben Creek Valley their home, as well as all being buried at Himmel's Church

Cemetery, starting with John, Arthur, and Percy Troutman, and continuing their legacy with Rahn and his children still calling this area their home and business epicenter.

Family tree roots of this Troutman branch:[37]

1. Peter Trautman, 1738/40–1809, md. Eva Elizabeth Meyer, ca. 1740-1814, the Mahantongo Valley Pioneers
2. Heinrich, 1764–1833, md. (1) Regina Tschopp,[38] 1778-ca. 1809, (2) Catherine Hain, 1774–1854
3. Peter, 1790–1854, md. Elizabeth Batteiger, 1788-1865
4. Danial, 1817–1880, md. Elizabeth Bush, 1822–1915
5. James Bush Troutman, 1844–1915, md. Lena Adams, 1840–1911
6. John, 1872–1947, md. (1) Emma Goodman,[39] 1872–1910, (2) Hattie E. Rebuck. 1884-1965
7. Arthur, 1901–1974, md. Lena Reed, 1905-1999
8. Percy R. Troutman, 1929–2018, md. Pauline Snyder, 1932–2019
9. Rahn and Traci Troutman
10. Kaitlyn Troutman

37. See the book *The Family of Peter Troutman and Eva Elizabeth Meyer, Mahantongo Pioneers* by Steve Troutman, published by Sunbury Press.

38. Rahn's ancestor.

39. Ibid.

Home of Troutman's Food Service, LLC previously the Percy Troutman Feed Mill

Kaitlyn (26), Kylie (19), Rahn (62), Traci (55), Connor (23) Troutman.

Rahn and Kylie Troutman. Kylie will be the future business owner.

Family of John Troutman Spouses and Children

Men in Back Row Standing (Left to Right): Lester Campbell, Arthur Troutman, Roy J. Troutman, B. Lloyd Smith, John Troutman, James D. Troutman, Harlan Klock, Clarence Curtiss Troutman.

Second Row (Left to Right): Standing: Katie N. (Troutman) Campbell, Melba V. Campbell (child in front of Katie); Seated: Lena (Reed) Troutman holding Derl A. Troutman, Tami (Troutman) Smith with J. Garwood Smith standing in front, Hattie (Rebuck) Troutman holding Bernice Klock, Florence B. (Troutman) Klock holding Gloria Klock with Annabell Klock standing to her left, Goldi Margaret (Kieffer) Troutman holding Lawrence Troutman

Front Row (seated on ground): Anna (Troutman) Boyer, Samuel J. Troutman.

This photograph is from the collection of Katie Troutman Campbell. Katie's siblings include Arthur Troutman, married to Lena Reed, and Tamie Troutman, married to Smith. Katie has written on the back of this photograph: Katie's father, John, Aunt Sara, and Uncle Frank Troutman. Rahn Troutman confirmed that Sara and Frank were John's brother and sister. John was Rahn Troutman's great-grandfather. Photo courtesy of Walker Marks of Downingtown, Pennsylvania. Walker's grandmother was Katie Troutman.

The John Troutman farm was located south of Himmel's Church where Middlecreek Road intersects Schwaben Creek Road. Reed Road intersects Middlecreek Road. Reed Road leads west to the top of the hill where the John Troutman farm was situated. It was on the south side of Reed Road.

John Troutman getting ready to do chores on the farm.

Clarence, Goldie (Kieffer), and Lawrence Troutman.

Clarence was born in 1900 and died in 1967. Lawrence Troutman later operated a dairy farm near the intersection of Wolfe and Schaffer Roads, Dornsife, Pennsylvania. This location is between Rebuck and Red Cross. Clarence is the son of John Troutman (1872–1947), married Emma Goodman (1872–1910).

A School in Slutter Valley

Daniel Wilkinson lives in the one-room school building and his mother, Diane, lives next door. The valley takes its name from the Pennsylvania Dutch word *schlutter*, which refers to spring onions. When onions are six inches high and suitable to pull and put on the table as spring onions, they are in *Schlutter*.

A School in Slutter Valley. Photos courtesy of Daniel Wilkinson and his mother Diane.

Neal and Diane built a home next to the one-room school. The Straubs lived next to the school before Neal and Diane. There is an artesian spring on Diane's property, which was the water source for the school. Goldie (Tressler) Wilkinson is in one of these photos as a student. Goldie married Alton Wilkinson. Goldie and Alton lived where Goldie grew up at the Mouse Creek Bridge north of the Urban Gap. The red brick one-room school has been covered with siding. Paul and Gladys Latsha and their two sons lived in the school building before the present owner, Daniel Wilkinson.

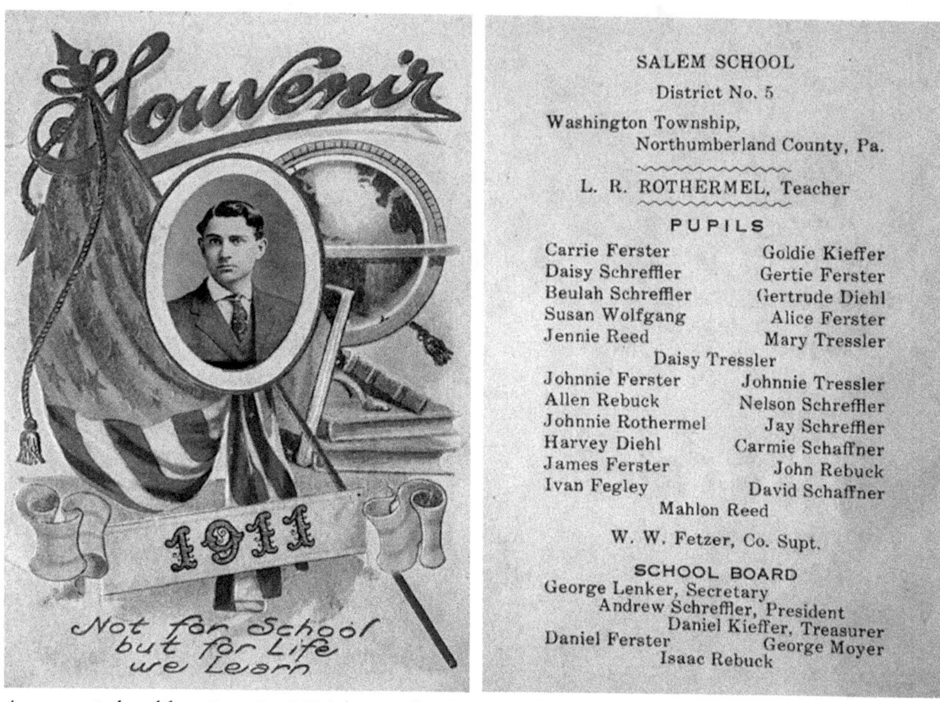

SALEM SCHOOL
District No. 5
Washington Township,
Northumberland County, Pa.

L. R. ROTHERMEL, Teacher

PUPILS

Carrie Ferster — Goldie Kieffer
Daisy Schreffler — Gertie Ferster
Beulah Schreffler — Gertrude Diehl
Susan Wolfgang — Alice Ferster
Jennie Reed — Mary Tressler
Daisy Tressler
Johnnie Ferster — Johnnie Tressler
Allen Rebuck — Nelson Schreffler
Johnnie Rothermel — Jay Schreffler
Harvey Diehl — Carmie Schaffner
James Ferster — John Rebuck
Ivan Fegley — David Schaffner
Mahlon Reed

W. W. Fetzer, Co. Supt.

SCHOOL BOARD
George Lenker, Secretary
Andrew Schreffler, President
Daniel Kieffer, Treasurer
Daniel Ferster — George Moyer
Isaac Rebuck

A souvenir booklet given in 1911 by teacher L.R. Rothermel, 24 students are named, including Mary, Daisy, and Johnny Tressler. Perhaps they were Goldie's older siblings. School #5.

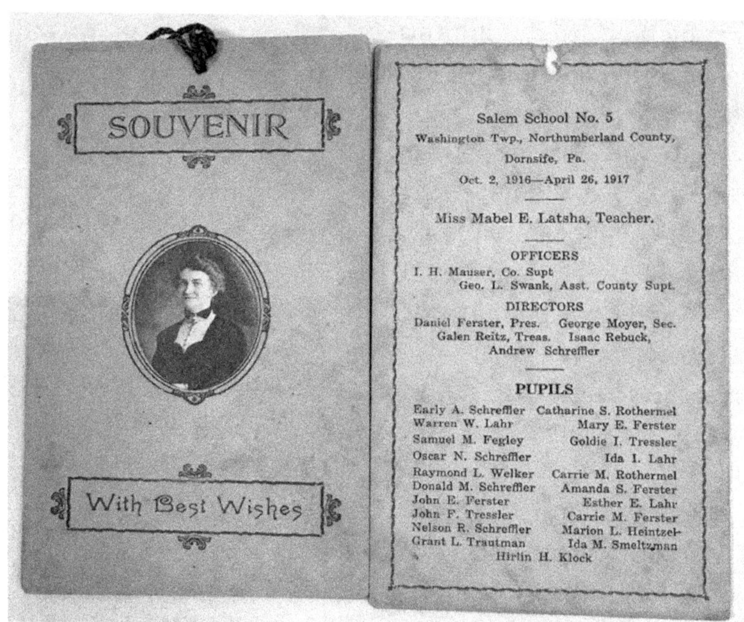

Salem School No. 5
Washington Twp., Northumberland County,
Dornsife, Pa.
Oct. 2, 1916—April 26, 1917

Miss Mabel E. Latsha, Teacher.

OFFICERS
I. H. Mauser, Co. Supt
Geo. L. Swank, Asst. County Supt.

DIRECTORS
Daniel Ferster, Pres. — George Moyer, Sec.
Galen Reitz, Treas. — Isaac Rebuck,
Andrew Schreffler

PUPILS
Early A. Schreffler — Catharine S. Rothermel
Warren W. Lahr — Mary E. Ferster
Samuel M. Fegley — Goldie I. Tressler
Oscar N. Schreffler — Ida I. Lahr
Raymond L. Welker — Carrie M. Rothermel
Donald M. Schreffler — Amanda S. Ferster
John E. Ferster — Esther E. Lahr
John F. Tressler — Carrie M. Ferster
Nelson R. Schreffler — Marion L. Heintzel-
Grant L. Trautman — Ida M. Smeltzman
Hirlin H. Klock

Goldie (Tressler) Wilkinson's Salem One Room School House Memorabilia.

School Souvenir from the One Room School #7. Given by teacher, Ralph Kline, in 1911.

Diane Wilkinson provided this information and school booklets collected by Goldie (Tressler) Wilkinson.

Catherine Straub, wife of Henry Straub, Jr., transferred a parcel of land to the Washington School District on the 23rd of April, 1870. This was for the establishment of Salem School #5. Goldie was born in 1909.

Goldie would have been six years old when a report card was issued to her by the teacher, Mary Reed, on September 13, 1915 (not pictured).

The souvenir booklet shown above was given by Miss Mabel E. Latsha, teacher, at Salem School #5 for the year October 2, 1916-April 26, 1917. Goldie I. Tressler is named as a pupil (age 8) as one of 21 students.

Young Man's Foresight Warrants Expansion[40]

A young Keystone State feedman is Percy R. Troutman, who operates feed supply businesses at Dornsife and Dalmatia. The story of the Troutman feed enterprises hinges on the fact that Troutman spent his early manhood on a farm. He attended Mahanoy Joint School and, on graduating, went to work with his father on the family farm. With practical experience and diligent reading, he acquired practical ideas on farm management. In 1947, Mr. Troutman carefully moved into the feed business.
In this section, farming is diversified. Commercial egg production is tops. Pork

40. Newspaper article ca. 1960, contributed by Rahn Troutman. Edited for publication.

production comes next, and dairying is in third position. His feed business grew and prospered. Troutman sensed the need for constantly changing his pattern of service to dovetail with a changing agriculture. His first major change was to offer grinding and mixing services. Farmers wanted to save labor and time of hauling their homegrown grains to a mill for grinding and mixing, and the return of the mixture to the farm. He purchased a Daffin mobile grinder and mixer in 1956. As time went on, Troutman decided that the handling of feed in bulk, was the answer to the growing demand of farmers to cut feeding costs. By inaugurating the bulk method of feed handling in hopper cars having mostly confined to feed crumbles and pellets, he has provided more efficient service to his customers. Dairy feeds containing up to twenty-nine percent molasses have been delivered in bulk to farms, without trouble.

Union School, Washington Township

Photo courtesy of Gayle Rebuck. This brick school was located west of the Village of Rebuck, near Red Cross on Schwaben Creek Road. The residence of Richard and Jeanne Adams is situated near the school location. The photo is from 1937. This building has been removed. Hilbert Paul, the father of Gayle Rebuck, stands in the back row, second to the right of the teacher. Sisters Corrine and Florence Paul are wearing black dresses with white collars, standing in Row 2, in front of the teacher. Sisters Lena Paul and Marvie Paul are wearing print dresses with white collars, standing in the second row next to Florence. Others in the photo include Mark and Guy Paul. Union School teachers included: 1931-32 Charles E. Baum; 1932-33 Mrs. Barron; 1935-36?; Harry Phillips 1937-38. Harry Phillips is in this picture.

Red Cross

The Village of Red Cross (formerly Mahanoy)

The Village of Red Cross is the gateway to the Schwaben Creek Valley. The Schwaben Creek joins the larger Mahanoy Creek about one mile northwest of the village. The Mahanoy Creek continues to Herndon, where it flows into the Susquehanna River. Very large gravel bars are found near Red Cross at the confluence of the Mahanoy and Schwaben Creeks. These gravel bars had their origin during the ice ages of the past.[41]

A modern highway, State Route 225, bypasses the village previously known as Mahanoy. County history books recount this area, named Mahanoy, as the mustering place for the local militia during the Revolutionary War. This militia was composed of citizen soldiers who practiced military activities here in the lowlands of the Schwaben Creek. Black powder guns were used for target practice in preparation for a British and Indian invasion from the north. Many of the forefathers of current valley residents participated in these events.

In an effort to document the local history, an interview with Connie Tressler was arranged on the 19th of January 2025. The scene illustrates the severity of a snowstorm on a Sunday afternoon. The history of this dwelling place is recorded on a bronze plaque visible from the highway passing in front of her home. The plaque reads as follows:

The residence of Connie Tressler, 19th of January 2025.

> The Farm at Red Cross, formerly, Mahanoy. On August 22, 1749, the government purchased land from the Indians extending from the Susquehanna River to the Delaware River. As far east as Line Mountain, the land on the west side was retained by the Indians. On March 25, 1751, by letter patent recorded in Patent Book 50-A, page 134, the land was

41. See the book *Geology of the Mahanoy, Mahantongo, and Lykens Valleys* by Steven E. Troutman, published by Sunbury Press.

deeded to George Adam Stump and was named 'Stump Town.' A joining tract of land was conveyed to Adam Kauble on May 30, 1795, in Patent Book 55, Page 435 and was known as 'Gables Hall'. Here, John Stump and Adam Kauble (a.k.a. Adam Gable) erected a building which served as an inn during the French and Indian War. Line Mountain served as the boundary between the two adversaries. In 1775, Northumberland County was established, with the southern portion known as Mahanoy Township. It was here that the militia for the lower part of Northumberland County trained during the Revolutionary War. The battalion muster for the southern part of Northumberland County was annually held here until the discontinuance of the old militia system. In 1784, the land to the north was conveyed to the government by the Indians. The present brick house was erected by John Kunsman and named Kunsman's Tavern. Thousands of immigrants heading to the new purchase passed by the tavern, which also served as a resting place for those travelling by stagecoach. Kunsman's Tavern was later remodeled by a subsequent owner and known for many years as the Smith Hotel. Its doors were closed as a public house in 1880. The house was restored to its current condition in 2004 by Connie Tressler.

This outbuilding, adjacent to the residence of Connie Tressler, is legendary. According to oral tradition, it was utilized by the militia as a storage place for gunpowder during the Revolutionary War.

The early settlement of Mahanoy, included St. Peter's Church, the school house (photo center), a lodge hall, (the large building between the school and the church), Rebuck's general store, later Tressler's general store and post office, (behind the trees, to the right of the school), and a small store named Lebo's Cellar, (lower right hand corner.

Sometime after the establishment of the postal system, a name change for the post office was requested. There were too many Mahanoys. Mahanoy City and Mahanoy Plane were so named, being located on the Mahanoy Creek in the eastern regions of Northumberland County. There was confusion with the Mahanoy of lower Northumberland County. A postal official visited the general store and post office in Mahanoy to speak with Mr. Isaac B. Tressler, the owner of the store and post office. Mr. Tressler was not in favor of a name change. The postal official persisted with his request. Mr. Tressler asked what name should be given to this post office, but the official did not offer any suggestions. After much deliberation, the postal official's eyes fell upon a tin can on the shelf, behind the general store counter. The tin can had a red cross on it, as it served as a storage place for bandages, which were sold in the store. The postal official proposed the name Red Cross to be the new name of this post office to replace the well-known name of Mahanoy.

Mrs. Isaac B. Tressler poses on her porch in Red Cross. She appears to be dressed for a special occasion. Her residence was located within the Village of Red Cross, near the location of the general store. Photo courtesy of Connie Tressler.

The General Store and Post Office in Mahanoy, now Red Cross. Isaac B. Tressler and men and boys pose on the front steps of the general store. The photo appears to be a three-generation picture with sons and grandsons. Isaac B. Tressler is seated on a tall stool in the center. Three men stand behind him. One man on the right is posing with his wife. The young boys next to Isaac are most likely his grandsons. The father of the grandsons is standing behind the boys. Photo courtesy of Connie Tressle.

Lloyd J. Tressler and Olive (Krebs) Tressler pose in front of their home in Herndon. This residence is across the street from Seibert's Church on Main Street. Photo courtesy of Connie Tressler.

Lloyd Jerome Tressler and Olive (Krebs) Tressler. Lloyd was born and raised in Red Cross. Lloyd married Olive Krebs. She was the daughter of Dr. Krebs who practiced medicine in Herndon. Dr. Kreb's medical office was later utilized by Attorney Isaac J. Tressler who practiced law in Herndon. The pose is in a photographer's studio. Photo courtesy of Connie Tressler.

St. Peter's Lutheran Church of Red Cross

The Citizen Standard newspaper, Valley View, Pennsylvania, August 22, 2024, records the 250th anniversary of St. Peter Lutheran and Reformed Church of Red Cross.[42] The following narrative is edited from this edition. An interview with Linda (Scheib) Boyer and Audrey (Smith) Eisenhower provided the following church photos. There were four different buildings associated with this congregation. The first was a schoolhouse-church and dwelling place. A large structure built of logs was the second church. A brick edifice with a large steeple on the west end was the third building. The present church, with a similar large steeple and bell tower on the east end, would be the fourth church building.

According to Bell's *History of Northumberland County*, St. Peter's Union Church, Lutheran and Reformed, is one of the oldest churches in the county. In the year 1774, a warrant was issued for a tract of land. On May 6, 1775, the tract of land was surveyed for Gotlieb Leffler and Henry Krebs, in trust for the Lutheran and Calvinist (Reformed) Church schoolhouse and contained 27 and three-quarters acres. Worshipping was held as early as 1774 in an irregular way, with only occasional preaching in those early days. The building was used for dwelling, school,

42. Author's note: *The Citizen Standard* newspaper account records the existence of three buildings solely erected for the use as a congregational meeting place in Red Cross. The same newspaper account gives reference to an earlier public meeting house, stating that a school-church dwelling place was established on church property with worship beginning in 1774. Worship in this public meeting house was in an irregular way with occasional preaching. Therefore, there were actually four buildings that were used for worship on the land that was purchased from the Penn Family.

and preaching purposes. It was 26 feet by 40 feet, and one-and-a-half stories high. The teacher lived in one part, and in the other, he taught school. First, he taught in the German language, and then in both German and English. In 1876, this building was repaired, and at that time it was used by the church sexton. The second church, a log building, was built about 1800. It was a two-story log building with a gallery on three sides and a pulpit on the other side, midway between the two floors. Between the years 1821 and 1822, it was weatherboarded and painted yellow. Both congregations used the church. They would take turns, one week Lutheran and the next week Reformed. It is believed that the wooden church sat in the middle of the current cemetery. In 1858, the records show that the wooden church was showing its age, and the brick church below was built in 1859. After the construction in 1859, the log church was removed.

Charter of the Evangelical Lutheran Congregation of St. Peter's Church, in Jackson Township, December 6, 1859. The Charter of Incorporation of St. Peter's Church names the following Persons Citizens of this Commonwealth viz: Isaac Reitz, Abraham Klock, George Lahr, George Snyder, David Eyster, David Latsha, Samuel Malich, Peter Ferster, Valentine Klock, Peter Klock, David Zartman, John Klock, and Solomon Dressler.

The cornerstone of the third church building of the St. Peter's congregation in Red Cross was set on June 12, 1859. It was written entirely in German and was placed by the Rev. Jacob Fritzinger, Reformed pastor and Reverend Augusta Bergner, Lutheran pastor. During the use of this church, in 1876, an organ valued at $340 was approved to be purchased and placed in the church for the use of both the Lutheran and Reformed congregations.

The church records show again that age has taken its toll on the brick church. Subsequently, a new brick church was built, incorporating the 1859 cornerstone with the addition of the new cornerstone dated 1914. Worship continues in this building today.

Two Room School, Red Cross, Pennsylvania

Photos courtesy of Rahn Troutman and Doyle Ferster.

This two-room schoolhouse at the intersection of Route 225 and Schwaben Creek Road was last used as a Line Mountain School District administration building. Rahn Troutman attended kindergarten in 1969. Kindergarten was held in one room on the east side. The other room on the west side was utilized by the school district's superintendent. After kindergarten was no longer held here, the school became an administration building. Scott Heim dated the removal of the building as July 2016. The schoolhouse was well constructed of tongue and groove boards covered by red brick.

Dr. Muth of Red Cross

Photo by Craig Troutman, January 2025.

Dr. Reuben Harris Muth (1826-1899) was a prominent resident of Red Cross in the Civil War and post-Civil War era. His residence was approximately one mile west of the village. He attended patients with house calls throughout the Schwaben Creek Valley and beyond. Muth Hill Road is named as a township road near his residence. This name commemorates his public service. Dr. Muth's residence, pictured above, is currently the home of Damien and Maria Malfara, with their children: Luke, Henry, and Eva.

Dr. Lawrence Knorr's dissertation was a full-length biography of Dr. Muth and a full accounting of his medical career. Dr. Knorr utilized an extant set of daybooks containing every appointment and fee charged. Dr. Muth attended the University of

Pennsylvania, where he received his medical training. He first practiced in Stumpstown, Lebanon County (now Fredericksburg). After the passing of his wife, he moved to Mahanoy, now Red Cross, at the outset of the Civil War. One of Dr. Muth's first patients was Louisa Deppen, the daughter of Abraham Deppen, one of the wealthiest men in the area. Dr. Muth and Louisa married not long after, in 1861. Dr. Muth served the Mahantongo Valley from 1861 to 1898.[43] He is buried at St. Peter's Church in the village.

Mahanoy Parish, Lutheran Church Parsonage

Mahanoy Parish, Lutheran Church Parsonage.

In 1907, the Mahanoy Parish included seven churches, all of which were established as Union Churches except St. John's of Pump Station, which was organized as a Lutheran Church. The Mahanoy Parish Union Churches included: Himmel's, at Rebuck; Zion in Herndon; St. Peters of Red Cross; Davids of Hebe; St. Paul's of Urban; and Immanuel of Hunter Station. This lovely brick home is located along Route 225, north of the Schwaben Creek, between the Villages of Red Cross and Pump Station.

An 1875 map of Washington Township, Northumberland County, identifies the dwelling at the top of this page as a Lutheran

43. See *A Saddlebag Doctor of the Mahantongo Valley* by Lawrence Knorr, Ph.D., published by Sunbury Press.

Lutheran Parsonage, Mahanoy Parish, 1875.

Former Mahanoy Parish Lutheran Church Parsonage. The parsonage has been remodeled to include a new front door and a larger porch. Photo January 19, 2026.

St. Johns Church, Pump Station.

parsonage. The location is at the intersection of Hooflander Road and Derle's Road, north of the Village of Urban. The ornately carved porch pillars were originally in the historic stone Himmel's Church. A photograph of Himmel's Church interior showing the "wine glass pulpit" also shows these pillars supporting the balcony in the sanctuary. The pillars were removed when the stone church was demolished to build a new church.

The 1858 map of Northumberland County shows a one-room school in the gap near this location. The school was located on the old Tulpehocken Path, which is now Hooflander Road. It was situated on the boundary line separating Jordan and Washington Townships, west of the bridge over Mouse Creek.

St. John's, at Pump Station, in Jackson township, was organized at the home of John S. Klock during the pastorate of Rev. J. F. Bayer, and a church was erected in 1885. It was dedicated in September of the same year and is exclusively Lutheran.

St. John's Evangelical Lutheran Church was a branch of the old St. Peter's Church in Red Cross. The church seen here was erected in 1885. Reverend D. M. Stetler took charge on the first of April 1887.

Zartman Homestead, near Pump Station

Henry Zartman owned these premises during the Revolutionary War. He served on the Committee of Safety, Mahanoy Township and painted this date, December 1, 1776, in second story of the spring house.

Henry Zartman homestead.

Salem (Zartman's) Church, Jackson Township, Northumberland County, Pennsylvania

Mahanoy (now Red Cross) served as the mustering place for the citizens' militia.

This congregation was a member of the United Evangelical Denomination. The brick church was erected in from 1861 to 1864. The church was established on Jacob Zartman's farm. There are three burial grounds near the church. One is directly in front of the church, where Jacob Sr. and son Henry are believed to repose. Both rendered service in the Revolutionary War. The church is west of the Village of Red Cross, near the intersection of Grively Hill Road and Township Road 3001. The community of Otto Station is nearby. Today, only the foundation stones remain. The photo is courtesy of Blanch Troutman, deceased.

Appendix A:
Something about Mahantongo Valley Mills, as Recorded in Other Sources

The Penn's Manor of Spread Eagle and the Grist Mills of the Upper Mahantongo Valley by Steve E. and Joan E. Troutman was published in 2015 by Sunbury Press Inc. Part I details the Spread Eagle Manor and the establishment of Klingerstown and the Klingerstown Grist Mill. Part II details the Klingerstown Mill. Part III describes the mills of the Upper Mahantongo Valley located in Schuylkill and Northumberland Counties. Copies are available from Steve E. Troutman or Sunbury Press.

History of Northumberland County, Pennsylvania by Herbert C. Bell, was published in 1891. It was reprinted by the Northumberland County Historical Society. This volume contains mill history with each chapter denoted by township:

Chapter XXII, Lower Augusta Township, p. 705. The De Witt Mill is the oldest in the township; here a mill was built toward the close of the last century by a Mr. Hilterbeil, from whom it passed successively to Christian Falk, Henry Masser, and Mr. De Witt, the present owner. He erected the present mill, a two-story frame structure in 1840; it is situated six miles from Sunbury, near the Harrisburg Road (Route 147) and derives its water–power from Hallowing Run. (Located north of Fisher's Ferry).

A mill was built on the Boyle's Run Road three miles from Fisher's Ferry in 1858, by John Snyder; he operated it until its destruction by fire in 1880.

Chapter XXIII, Upper Mahanoy Township, p. 710. The mill now operated at Leck Kill Post Office by William Kehres, was built by a Mr. Schenckweiler. It is furnished with three sets of buhrs (millstones). (Geist General Store and post office was built by Peter Beisel in 1825 as a tavern. This stone tavern, which still stands in the center of Leck Kill, was located adjacent to this mill.)

Samuel Rothermel's mill on Mahantongo Creek at the line between Northumberland and Schuylkill Counties was built by Daniel Herb. (It is lately recalled as Stehr Brothers' Mill.)

Chapter XXIV, Lower Mahanoy Township, p. 712. The Witmer Mill (in Dalmatia), as originally built by George Brosius, was a log structure; the present frame building is three stories high, equipped with three sets of buhrs. The mill now operated by Michael Spotts was built in 1845 by Michael Wert and Michael Rudel. (Dalmatia was earlier known as Georgetown.)

Chapter XXVIII, Little Mahanoy Township, p. 735. In the assessment of 1814, John Dunkelberger, Sr., is credited with a grist and saw mill on Mahanoy Creek; Abraham Rothermel, with a grist, saw, and oil mill on Mahanoy Creek, and Conrad Raker, with a saw mill on Little Mahanoy Creek. At the present time, there are two mills in the township, one at Dornsife and the other owned by A. S. Speece, who also operates a powder mill. (The gunpowder mill was located east of Hunter Station on the lower road.)

Chapter XXX, Jackson Township, P. 744. If traditional information can be credited, a mill was in operation on Mahanoy Creek in this township as early as 1785. The site is a mile and a half north of Herndon, and the building, a dilapidated stone structure, is now owned by David Bohner. It was erected by Abraham McKinney. Henry Zartman and P. Troutman are named as residents prior to 1776. (At this time, Jackson Township was larger than it is today.)

In 1809, William Dobson built a mill at the site of C.W. Dewitt's; it was subsequently rebuilt by Jacob Gonsar and furnished with three sets of buhrs. Reuben Weiser afterward operated it until 1822, when it was purchased by W. W. Dewitt, father-in-law of the present proprietor. It is situated at the Mahanoy Post Office (Red Cross 2024).

Kobel's Mill, a three-story brick structure located on Mahanoy Creek at the gap in Line Mountain, was built in 1855 by Jonathan Dunkelberger. It is furnished with a turbine wheel and three sets of buhrs. The present owner is Henry Kobel. (Many recall this as Bohner's Mill, near Dornsife.)

Chapter XXXV, Jordan Township, p. 773. The Wert Mill, a three-story frame and stone structure, is situated in the extreme northwestern part of the township. (Mandata) It was originally established 100 years ago (1791).

Chapter XXXVIII, Washington Township, p. 787. Keihl Brothers' Mill is situated near Rebuck Post Office, on Greenbrier Creek (Schwaben Creek). The first mill on this site was erected during the early settlement of the township; it was replaced in 1838 by the present building, a frame structure furnished with two sets of buhrs, and capable of grinding ten barrels of flour per day. William Kehres purchased the property from a Mr. Knobel in 1830 and rebuilt the mill in 1838 (near Rebuck Post Office-Drumheller's Store.)

Latsha Brother's Mill was built in 1819 by Daniel Gonsar, who erected at the same time a saw mill; the latter has not been in operation for some years. (Village of Rebuck, Pennsylvania)

One of the Rebuck family built a saw mill near Rebuck Post Office, about 1815; it has been abandoned for many years.

Andrew G. Brosius's Mill, also on Greenbrier (Schwaben) Creek, was originally erected by the father of the present owner. It is especially adapted to the manufacture of linseed oil, but chopping is also done. (Linseed oil is derived from flax. Greenbrier Creek is a tributary of Schwaben Creek. It flows north and joins Schwaben Creek in the center of the Village of Greenbrier. The old

Brosius Mill at the center of this village was operated by Hen Brosius. This mill was most recently known as Snyder's Mill. The Snyder's Mill building, constructed of cement blocks, was recently torn down.)

Henry Fisher established a foundry at Rebuck in 1870 for the manufacture and repair of plows and other agricultural implements. It is now operated by W. H. Fisher.

Mr. Bell describes Rebuck as follows: The post village of this name is situated near the center of Washington Township. The first post master was Godfrey Rebuck, in whose honor the office was named. The Village comprises two stores, two hotels, blacksmith and wagon shops, the mill of Keihl Brothers, and the foundry of W. H. Fisher, with perhaps a dozen private residences.

The Village of Rebuck pictured on a calendar advertising F. L. Kehres and son.

About the Authors

Steve and Joan became acquainted in high school. Their marriage in 1975 was celebrated with a trip to Bermuda. The honeymoon destination was suggested by a travel agent Joan visited in Shamokin, PA during her lunch hour. It was indeed a beautiful place. This was Steve's first plane ride. In 1975, 50 plus years ago, most passengers followed an implied dress code. Men wore ties and jackets; women wore dresses or pant suits.

In 2025, Steve and Joan celebrated their 50th wedding anniversary, with another trip to Bermuda. The island provides vacationers with rest and relaxation. Tourists do not drive cars. Public transportation and motor bikes are the means of transportation for visitors.

The moon gate pictured here is a unique architectural structure found throughout the island. It is seen on public and private land. The moon gate's circular shape represents wholeness and eternity.

www.ingramcontent.com/pod-product-compliance
Lightning Source LLC
LaVergne TN
LVHW080248110826
845148LV00023BA/867
9798888192627